The Law of Attraction Meets Financial Stewardship

Bridging the Intangible & Tangible with
Practical Tips and Guidance to
Support Your Ongoing Financial Abundance © 2015

LAURIE BONSER, CFP™CPA

Working with Laurie: *Client Comments*

'Laurie is passionate about her profession. She is never short on quick tips to help a client manage or navigate an issue. Her long-term experience as a planner is unmistakable given her depth of knowledge on any given topic.'

'Thank you for the wonderful workshop. I learned so many useful things. I started reading your book and I really liked it. What a wonderful gift you gave us yesterday.'

'Thank you for your very informative session last night. I appreciate the hard work you put into guiding women through different phases of our lives.'

'This wonderful person has tremendous experience and insight when it comes to helping you plan for your future. Worth every minute spent with her!'

'I don't know if there are many people out there that do what you do, but I am grateful to have found you! I am so unsure of so many things right now, it's a comfort to work with someone that looks at every aspect of a client's circumstances not just the financial picture. I was struck by how you seemed to pick up on things we hadn't actually mentioned, like my resistance to listen to what the universe has been trying to tell me for many years. My biggest obstacle is fear, so what I am hoping for going forward is that you stick with me through my confusion and possible resistance to certain 'scary' new concepts...together we can chip away at that 'thick skull' of mine.'

'Laurie creates a very sacred, comfortable space that allows you to feel open and balanced. Her office holds a relaxing atmosphere while maintaining the necessary qualities of professionalism. I would highly recommend her to anyone. Thank you for your compassionate services, Laurie!'

'When I came to Laurie I was feeling very anxious and ungrounded. There were many things going on career wise for me, and I was having a hard time feeling settled down in one or two particular areas. Laurie has a very calming presence about her, and worked with me to focus on just a few areas that I would nurture, vs trying to do everything. She did some energy work on me as well. After the session I felt more centered and relaxed. She also gave me some

tools to use at home to help me re-center. I highly recommend Laurie's services. She is one amazing practitioner.'

'I just wanted to touch base with you regarding your energy work. Since my visit, I've felt like a new woman. I think I had a vibrational shift of some sort, because my outlook has been so very different. Granted, I still have my days, but overall I've been in much better spirits. Thanks so much for your help last night. That session was very powerful.'

Dedication

Endless gratitude to all those supportive spirits, both earthly and universal, who empower us with love, discernment, and community.

Table of Contents

Setting the Stage

I'm writing here for those motivated people who want to replace the energy-sapping fear and stress of typical financial conversations and decisions with the *good vibrations* and healthy, thoughtful, long-term intentions associated with an abundance focus. This guide is designed as a compliment to the Law of Attraction (Abraham Hicks) principles provided by Esther and Jerry Hicks (www.AbrahamHicks.com) and the abundance message offerings of other noted spiritual voices including Lazaris (www.lazaris.com), Seth (Jane Roberts), and Frank (Tracy Farquhar).

These overarching principles of attraction, abundance, and universal connections are our inspirations and aspirations. The sole purpose of this written offering is to help you build a tangible framework for your earthly financial-related endeavors that is capable of fully supporting your whole journey within these principles. We will not be focusing here on a myriad of details or specific 'how' technical solutions, which are counter to effectively combining our earthly pursuits with universal synchronization in our highest and best interests. Rather, the repeated messages will concentrate on the very productive ways we can strengthen our inner intuitions, personal connections, and conscious choices to become higher vibrational individuals experiencing greater fulfillment, peace, and purpose.

*"The important subject of money and financial success is not the 'root of all evil' as many have quoted – nor is it the path to happiness. However, because the subject of money touches most of you in one way or another hundreds or even thousands of times every day, it is a large factor in your vibrational makeup and in your personal point of attraction. So when you are able to successfully control something that affects most of you all day, every day, you will have accomplished something rather significant. In other words, because such a high percentage of your thoughts in any given day reside around the topic of money or financial success, as soon as you are able to deliberately guide your thoughts, not only is it certain that your financial success must improve, but the evidence of that success will then prepare you for deliberate improvement in every aspect of your life experience." -- **Abraham Hicks**

This book provides the very practical ideas, new perspectives, and guidance needed to support and maintain the financial abundance and quality of life you desire as part of the overall commitment to your spiritual journey and growth. The format consists of short labeled sections and chapters for ease of reading and reference. And it can easily serve as a daily resource when facing financial decisions and situations.

I was inspired and guided to combine a unique variety of professional and personal experiences to create and share this 'bridge' of information as a heartfelt contribution to our respective journeys. So my intention is to coach you to fish in your own expanding stream instead of providing a set mantra of steps, accomplishments, or success measurements…the latter which might at first seem comforting or attention-catching, but actually produce a man-made, lowest common denominator result.

"My purpose is not to solve your problems for you, but to put you in touch with your own power. My purpose is not to come between you and your own freedom by giving you answers, even to the most tragic of problems. My purpose is to reinforce your own strength, for ultimately the magic of your being is well equipped to help you find fulfillment, understanding, exuberance, and peace." -- **Seth**

There were three primary reasons I was compelled to offer the first guide on Financial Stewardship in 2014:

1) I seek to be part of the process for healing the fear and misinformation of how we often view and handle the area of finances in our lives.

2) I am engaged to raise the awareness of why financial stewardship is a vital part of our lives and how it is very much affects many other areas such as relationships, health, lifestyle, raising children, leaving a legacy, and supporting all our intentions and purpose.

3) I am charged to be a catalyst for people to empower themselves in this area and consequently gained greater power and fulfillment in all aspects of life.

For this new book in 2015, there was a fourth reason:

4) I am inspired and guided by personal study and spiritual experiences to offer this 'bridge translation' to help us more effectively and fully understand how to support the overarching financial abundance principles already provided by Abraham's message and that of many other spirit teachers by *focusing on how to implement practical, personal, ongoing financial decisions in ways that support our overall higher vibrational intentions and growth.*

After Financial Stewardship was published, I received many requests for additional specific examples to be used by people when teaching themselves these new approaches and testing out different decision making habits. So the scenarios and situations included in each section represent real life stories for the purpose of stimulating new thought processes and consideration of options in your own life; they are not intended to be rules for copying verbatim.

We can all visualize the image of an ocean representing endless abundance and imagine the sensation of floating in a feeling of fulfillment and refreshment. However, if we don't have a practical method for converting that resource (salt water) into a consumable element (fresh water), then we are not able to consume those benefits on a human basis. So, you're going to learn how to create your own de-salination tool for earthly financial life to do your own personal part in co-creating the delivery of the desired abundance. And even if you already have a figurative in-house plumbing structure existing for fresh water, the system has to be in the 'on' position with any obstructions (such as cracks, old roots, or sediments) cleared to receive the complete free flow of benefit. It's all about actively manifesting the results, not stopping part way at the envisioning stage.

This process is also much like a spider weaving a web: individual, fine strands are put into place one by one, but each stage creates a stronger, longer lasting form. And the ultimate goal of the spider's creation is to obtain their expected sustenance and nourishment.

A Different Approach

Many financial self-help approaches are tied to achieving a man-made ideal (how much is in your bank account), setting up process as a battle with winners and losers (there's a lack of resources out there so you better grab yours now), changing yourself (there must be something wrong with you if you aren't already rolling in money), try harder and focus (your persona is weak so toughen up your mind and use logic), or you need a proven structure or method in your life to follow (you are not capable of figuring this out on your own, so copy this special method).

From my perspective, these models all contribute toward weakening our own personal power, distancing ourselves from our unique individual purposes, removing the personal accountability portion of co-creation, and steering us back to competing and comparing between ourselves and other human beings.

When you believe that your ultimate connection is with God, Spirit, a universal consciousness, or other moniker, why lower your sights and diminish your power to meet a human measurement? Our ingredients tag doesn't say 'created with 20% real spirit; 80% unknown by-products.' We were created fully as divine beings and are 100% universal souls having a physical body (human) experience in this particular timeframe. The authentic personal measuring stick boils down to being in sync with your true self and your vibrational counterparts. And we don't need to depend on a more credentialed or more authoritative-sounding outside intermediary to find ourselves and validate that synchronization.

Using an affirmations approach, whether through daily cards or particular rituals, can definitely help support positive thoughts and new focuses. And I certainly encourage you to use whatever tools and combinations from other sources that feel helpful in reaching your goals.

However, if and when you feel stymied by confusion and anxiety as you actually address daily financial conversations and decisions (or you routinely avoid the subject altogether), then the targeted information and examples of Financial Stewardship are also available here to help bridge that gap between your sincere intentions and your current tool set and skills. *Aligning these resources means that you will fully leverage all the powerful aspects of your mind, body, and soul in your life's journey.*

Getting Out of Resistance and Endless Loops

So why do people get stuck or feel they can't practically manifest the tangible goals the financial abundance messages? The following are some of the reasons given to express their frustrations and current state of concern:

- Feeling a need to make or discover perfect choices

- An inability to quiet their mind and focus productively

- Inexperience with financial matters that generates lack of confidence and action

- Fear of losing current assets by making a wrong financial decision

- Mistaking wishes and affirmations for intention and action

- Trying a different approach a few times but not getting the specific outcome they wanted

- Seeking future abundance without acknowledging harmful current behaviors

- Substituting 'generally accepted' norms for their own intuitive choices

- Mistaking must-do meditation time with authentic spiritual conversation

- Feeling discouraged because the asked for item or timing was not received as expected

- Reducing their options with complicated requirements

- Fear of stepping into their own true roles if they do actually receive financial resources

We'll cover these blocking points in greater detail as we move through the book, but for the moment please consider the following section:

As part of the Hay House World Summit 2015 there was a wonderful interview between Esther Hicks and Reid Tracy discussing Abraham as 'collective consciousness' being interpreted. One of the first points that came across was this message:

"Money ties to everything, so negative focuses multiply the negative vibrational proportion to all areas of your life."

Other key points provided were:
- ✓ Put your emphasis on Joy versus a 'quest for growth'
- ✓ Vibrational reality (unconditional acceptance) precedes manifestation
- ✓ The state of allowing is the receiving state
- ✓ Forgiveness releases excesses and reasons to lower vibrations
- ✓ Words don't teach, experiences do
- ✓ Effective does not equal perfection
- ✓ The closer to the vibrational level of who you are, the more access you have to abundance
- ✓ Start practicing, build your new muscle strength
- ✓ Tithing should actually be a demonstration of abundance, sharing, appreciation, and gratitude…obligation doesn't work in vibrational work
- ✓ Finding yourself supersedes changing yourself

To reach the higher vibrational state and synchronicity embodied in these messages, we need to practice the Mind/Body/Soul balance in every decision making process we encounter. We're looking to create true core changes here ~ soul-generated riches that filter into all aspects of our lives rather than just mind-generated physical manifestations. Suspending the commonly accepted 'rational' and 'logical' expectations is part of the equation (really, whose expectations are they anyway?) Each individual needs to define and intuit their own purpose and areas of attraction.

As neuroscience and quantum physics are now proving with quantitative measurements, when we consciously take responsibility and choose to apply our own energy in focused ways that tie into our highest and best good, then changes can be made down to the very cellular levels of our bodies. Adjustments that were once thought by many to be either impossible or having a long manifestation time are now recognized to be very possible and sometimes instantaneous. Being committed to addressing all ongoing issues and choices in the same mindset of feeling good, reducing stress, and incorporating freedom and flexibility always ties back into the overarching messages of vibrational ease and synchronization.

Some of the wealthiest people in the world from a visible material standpoint are the least happy and most stressed about money, have little knowledge and discipline in financial matters, make harmful choices, and repeat painful cycles. Others are often in a defensive emotional mode, feeling the need to whip out a loaded personal resume every day to justify their significance or present a financial scorecard to prop up self-esteem. Why reach for a financially material abundant state you envisioned and then lose it because you didn't know how to continue to apply the abundance principles in specific decision making contexts?

First Steps

Okay, great concept in theory I hear you say, but how do I actually step away from all the personal and cultural norms about finances that are not really in my best interests? What new viewpoints can replace the old ones I've been taught?

There are two vital tools we need to consider carefully before moving forward specifically into the financial realm: Meditation and Awareness.

Meditation

When I myself first learned about this word many years ago, the impression presented to me was that of a person remaining in certain very specific physical poses that were generally uncomfortable at best – painful at worst – using only very specific chants and breathing methods. It was taught as a process to change yourself from an undisciplined, unworthy, unconnected person into one who surrendered to physical discomfort for the benefit of enlightenment and salvation. This process would take a long time to master, and even then it was uncertain if the higher benefits could be obtained if proper form and routine weren't followed precisely.

Speaking as one who had trouble sitting still for extended periods of time, did not have much patience to learn someone else's routine, and wasn't willing to wait an undetermined period of time for results, I tossed out the concept of 'meditation' pretty quickly. I basically figured that if you weren't a monk sitting on a stone in the middle of nowhere or a rigorous fitness devotee, there was little chance of attaining a higher state of grace through this method. Besides, it wasn't very inspirational to begin with the impression that I would be starting from an 'unworthy' or 'deficit' position right from the get-go…not a recipe for emotional success in anyone's book.

Since I could not fit into the meditation hallmark of that traditional teaching, I felt like was walking away from a sanctioned portal which held access to the meaning of life. But the particular exposure I had at the time to the process was completely out of sync with me for many reasons, and so for a while I ended up 'throwing the baby out with the bath water' in effect because of the method emphasis.

If your introduction to meditation was different from mine and you have already had wonderful experiences through this path, I am so happy for you (and apologies to those other practitioners I did not know at the time who taught differently). Keep doing whatever is working for you and adjust over time as guided for more learning and connections.

For those of you who had similar experiences to mine, or have not yet found a way that is really conducive to help quiet your mind, listen to your higher self, and converse with spirit helpers and guides, I offer some different ideas and suggestions for you to consider.

Regardless of your particular situation, being able to move into this different state of mind, in your own unique way, is critical to discovering your true needs and creating your new intentions for abundance in relationships, health, finances, work purpose, and all other areas that are important to you.

Contrary to my first experience long ago, I've since come to embrace my own style of meditation in the light of introspection, reflection, self-examination, pondering, quiet time, and concentrated conversations. Some of the resources I use to set the stage for my own dedicated meditation times include being in (or close to) a nature environment, relaxing music, a comfortable chair/blanket/piece of ground, breathing and stretching, holding a stone or crystal, expressing gratitude to guides and helpers, counting my many life blessings, and soaking in mother nature's healing energy. Other times during the day, it's a matter of just consciously shifting into the intention and spiritual connection on a focused basis for a particular use, as I seek to keep a constant thread available to help me in my personal purposes.

Whether you find you are most comfortable in a favorite chair, on a yoga mat, in bed, or sitting on the ground, then simply take that location that has positive associations for you and go with it. If having flowers or plants around helps, then place some greenery near your chosen place. Add music or stones or aromas as you prefer. Some people walk in a peaceful and safe place for some of their meditation time or perhaps floating in a kayak or raft in a quiet pond will become another option for you.

When you are starting to explore your own quiet time, consider beginning with 10-15 minutes set aside and anticipate that you will willingly look forward to extending this special time as your confidence and new muscles build. The interconnection between nature (grounding) and spiritual conversation (discovery) allows us to draw strength from each and more easily alternate back and forth from a place of increasing balance.

Once you have a comfortable physical location to use, the next key step is to gently experiment to learn how best to begin to quiet and focus your mind. This area often seems most daunting for people, but I encourage you to be compassionate with yourself and view this as a chance to create more mental and emotional muscle gradually over time as you practice. As the term practice implies, it will take some time and space to gain proficiency and clarity.

It is often effective to begin with a focus on your breathing patterns, as our life sustaining breaths reflect the basic essence of how we are responding at the moment. Check in with yourself: Are you taking more frequent, shallow breaths? Slower, deeper ones? Uneven, changeable patterns? When do your breathing characteristics change throughout the day?

What feedback does this awareness provide you? Do you feel better or more balanced in a particular rhythm? Spend a little time consciously choosing the physical pattern that provides you with better focus and relaxation. Use this as the starting point for your specially designated time. With some repetition you will find your breathing throughout the day takes on more qualities of your chosen pattern, and the benefits you previously just experienced during that one point in your day begin to manifest more often and with increasing regularity. You may also find attending a local gentle yoga class, guided meditation, gong bath, singing bowl or other special musical event will stimulate your interest and jump start your commitment and exploration.

During your early meditations, remember that although you may seemingly have hundreds of thoughts racing through your conscious mind when you begin, you do not have to act upon any one of them and can choose to say, 'I'll just let that one pass by.' You are not the sum of your thoughts or feelings, not good or bad, smart or silly, impossible or incapable. I personally believe the process of allowing thoughts and feelings to flow through your mind, instead of trying hard to block and judge them, helps express gratitude to the mind for the helpful services it does provide for us. We gradually build our ability to concentrate and focus for increasingly longer periods of time in the long run. If you don't argue with your mind and instead add in gratitude and love, then over time your very cells will lose the desire and prior rewards for obsessive, negative reactions and your thoughts will include far more beneficial and open characteristics. *Any time you choose a path that reduces resistance and allows energy to move with ease is one more opportunity to increase your vibrational level and heal more quickly.*

The end result of your meditation process, in whatever unique form you design for yourself, is to have authentic, clarifying, and empowering conversations with your deeper self and other divine messengers who are available to assist in your discovery time. These conversations are not about bragging rights, as in "I've done meditation for 20 years' or 'I meditate for an hour each day' or some other comparison with someone else's routines. If you treat meditation as an accomplishment, then that only reflects our cultural emphasis on <u>doing</u> and ticking one more thing off our list of 'should do's.' I've met any number of people who've proudly announced that they've *done meditation* for many years yet unfortunately their lives are no less filled with anger or illness or frustration than when they first started because of this very reason.

It's only when we move beyond the 'should do,' 'have to,' 'expected to,' and 'have done' phrases that we can get to the core of the real sticking points that are holding us back...old emotions, dependencies on others, personality labels, anger, fear, conformity, etc. As you get more comfortable with, and accepting of, all aspects of yourself from the past and in the present, you will then become increasingly free to identify the true motivations and intentions you have for the future.

Having these conversations with yourself and divine guidance are quite literally discussions: questions followed by listening for answers and options, hearing feedback that you perhaps didn't expect but needed to receive, and being as receptive as you possibly can be to whatever messages you get at any given moment.

Even during those times when you really think you aren't 'hearing anything' or getting information, you are most certainly helping to set a new course for your future life by the more open attitude and intentions you are expressing. It may be that you need time in actual physical sleep (unconscious mind) or a period of hours or days to recognize how new answers and information being shared with your conscious mind. Reminding yourself to stay relaxed and grateful will help particularly during your initial meditation conversations, and help ensure that they are meaningful and encouraging times for you. And being aware that you may receive answers in a variety of ways will keep you on your toes to pay attention to seeming coincidences, synchronicities, special signs, and experiences with 'human angels' who share a smile, kind word, or helpful suggestion with you.

Moving in your higher vibrational sphere and making choices in your best interests are the hallmarks of the true core changes that occur across your mind, body, and soul. You will experience increasingly more harmony and coordination with human relationships, your physical health, your companion animals, your view of nature and the weather patterns, and the flow of daily life (for example: driving, traffic, work schedules, chores, and family activities).

As you spend greater lengths of time in these new patterns, you will know that past 'negative' experiences cannot repeat again the same ways in your life – that you have adjusted your 'radio station' or 'television channel' to a new frequency and viewing mode. *Different outcomes based on your new conscious choices and actions are in the making,* and you will experience more fluid motion up to, and between, the higher emotional states that encompass peace, comfort, ease, purpose, flexibility, curiosity, fulfillment, and joy.

To assist you with your meditations, please also see the added BONUS section at the end of the book for the 44 Word and Message Card Deck.

Awareness

Several years ago I spent a great deal of concentrated time studying with natural horsemanship teachers to build a stronger, deeper relationship with my horse. Actually, my motivation initially was to try to figure out why the heck we figuratively kept banging heads together and why he didn't 'get me' and vice versa! I really wanted to have fun, compatible times with him, but somehow we just kept getting farther from that goal day by day, and it was breaking my heart.

Not surprisingly in retrospect, it was me who needed to make the most adjustments. But it was surprising that the eventual successes actually came from getting away from almost all the behaviors and methods I had been taught by many riding professionals since I was a young girl. Once I heard from these other 'natural horse teachers' that my own intuition and observations were actually spot on – and learned more about how and why horses are coming from a different perspective than we humans – the changes in our interactions were quickly and dramatically obvious for both of us. As I continued to raise my level of awareness and focus, became comfortable with my own core and skills, and was able to relax into a true partnership mode with him, his responses became so much more patient, accommodating, and interactive – and he was so relieved that his person finally got better educated and 're-programmed'!

One of the most important steps I learned and implemented was understanding the process of how we move along the horsemanship learning spectrum from Pat Parelli's presentations. Pat offered the following progression outline for horsemanship purposes, but it has proven very applicable in many other life ventures as well:

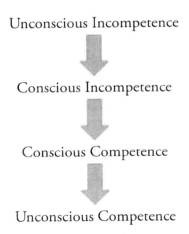

Unconscious Incompetence

Conscious Incompetence

Conscious Competence

Unconscious Competence

We begin many experiences unaware that we don't know what is going on around us or what impact our actions are having on a situation. As a result, we have no clue that there's a problem looming or that we're creating a less than desirable outcome. This is the *Unconscious Incompetence* state.

At some point, we realize that things just aren't going the way we wish they would or there is a definite reaction one day that stops us in our tracks and shouts "there's something really wrong and you need to pay attention right now." This is the *Conscious Incompetence state – or the Awareness phase*.

If we've taken the catalyst situation to heart and begun reaching out for information, connection, and intention to change to a more meaningful or desired outcome, then we enter the *Conscious Competence* mode and we are practicing new responses and building new mental, emotional, and physical skills.

With time and dedication, our new literal and figurative muscle tone allows us to manifest new results along our path with a natural ease, flow and beneficial outcome…the *Unconscious Competence state*. Maintaining this most beneficial state involves being aware at the 'un-ease level' – the beginnings of any imbalances or call for new action…well before reaching the stages where full blown illnesses or accidents manifest to get our attention. Making smaller adjustments sooner by addressing symptoms diverts more intense situations from developing and minimizes negative energies and resulting ripples. Small amounts of discomfort or stress can easily be cleansed regularly; critical situations take much more time and outside assistance.

If you have picked up this book at this time in your life, then you have reached the Conscious Incompetence/Awareness stage or have already some dedicated time to move into a new level of financial Conscious Competence. As you continue to journey along this spectrum, you will experience increased vibrational ease and energy and increasing abundances. It is my intention to assist you wherever possible with some new information, options, and support. Be patient and supportive of your beginning efforts, as we all have to start new skills in small steps. You too will have your moments or days of getting tangled up figuratively (as I quite did literally while gaining proficiency with 22 foot and 40 foot equine rope lines) but you will make great strides. Keeping a journal of your explorations and results will help remind you just how far you've developed in your awareness levels, skill sets, and the results of your new conscious choice process.

Money in Meditations

Sometimes we have a habit of thinking that it's an 'either or' situation between spirituality and money: if you consciously focus on money then you are taking attention away from your spiritual growth, or if you are really spiritually committed then there's no need to divert your path by delving into such a messy or potentially corrupting subject matter. Or perhaps we are hooked on the overall idea of abundance and plenty but then distance ourselves from the day-by-day personal choices we have available that would otherwise bring us to our stated goals of freedom and relaxation. As we reviewed earlier, though, when we view money as a resource tool available to apply in ways of care, sustenance, and purpose, then giving appropriate attention to the subject makes a great deal of sense in synchronizing and harmonizing our earthly experiences.

To successfully meld both areas, it's necessary to reinforce some new paradigms for yourself. Making this change involves bucking some very well entrenched and pervasive cultural, family, and institutional mantras.

*So I offer to you the **Money in Meditation 100% Challenge**: 100% in-the-moment gratitude while being 100% committed to new manifestations.*

The Zen tradition of this approach is known as "Wu Wei" or the art of doing without doing, working without working. By being totally in our own energy and being totally relaxed, we are not attached to a specific outcome and can set our intentions on building a new world while in acceptance of what is right now.

Throughout the book you will come across the following meditation at various points to help refocus your new efforts and perception changes. I hope that these words will generate the energy vibrations and intentions that are genuinely yours and genuinely rewarding.

Financial Abundance Opening Meditation

- I come to this moment open to new insights, guidance, and ideas, that will help me personally move into my own unique purposes.

- I agree to acknowledge and experience any challenging thoughts, feelings and emotions that arise now,

- Letting them flow on past - And to understand that I am not the sum of my past fears or experiences.

- I commit to remain open to the universal love and intuition available here,

- And to absorb increasing quantities of that love and trust into myself day by day.

- I come prepared today to actively learn and take my own steps in co-creating the abundance intended for me;

- And I trust that the information and resources I need will be provided through this state of awareness.

- I give thanks for all the many blessings already in my life,

- And am especially grateful for the spirits here now to assist me in my discoveries.

- So Be It.

Financial Stewardship Defined

Before we continue into the more financial-specific sections, I'd like to first share my personal definition of financial stewardship with you – as first published in *Financial Stewardship: A Guide for Personal Financial Health and Wellness (2014)*.

Personal financial stewardship is the care, conservancy, planning, attention, upkeep, and management of our financial resources and choices beginning at the individual level. (In contrast, Thesaurus.com shows ignorance, negligence, squandering, and waste as antonyms of stewardship.)

More importantly, financial stewardship represents a new way of considering our relationship with money, abundance, and using these tools for our authentic purposes. Just as with wildlife or environmental stewardship, the focus shifts to our roles as human guardians and managers of special gifts and resources that have been provided to us in the universal realm.

Please note: this definition does <u>not</u> limit financial stewardship to those being math wizards, those having professional credentials in the financial or business world, or to people labeled as analytical, objective, or left-brain thinkers. Nor is there any predetermined range or measure of financial wealth (or perceived lack thereof) that removes the responsibility of attention from being on the ball with stewardship in this area. We're all in the same learning boat together here and everyone needs to claim their personal responsibility and abilities for their own financial stewardship.

Financial stewardship has many components, including:

- Managing all of our current resources with wisdom

- Teaching our children about finances

- Integrating career choices with compensation possible

- Planning to make a family or charitable legacy gift

- Educating ourselves with knowledge from reliable sources

- Making thoughtful, conscious choices between options

- Considering how and why our decisions impact those around us

- Removing the fears and myths and masks that stymie our intentions

- Understanding the relationship between money and other areas of our lives

- Taking personal accountability for how we gather and use our financial resources – money, tangible assets, human capital (earnings potential), time, legacies, and more

- Invoking universal abundance with respect and responsibility

- Learning to view money as a currency, a tool, without judgment labels attached

- Becoming more adept at valuing our own time and contributions, and those of others around us

- Realizing that the awakenings and awareness in each of us of the wondrous universal gifts brings a calling to balance all areas of our lives, including financial stewardship

Integrating this new definition and holistic thought process with the Laws of Attraction messages is the practical application bridge connection that so far has been an elusive link for many otherwise sincere and motivated people, myself included for a number of years.

As we all become more comfortable and proficient in navigating this bridge route, the newly developed energies surrounding money and finances will flow beyond ourselves and into our entire cultural experience and outcomes. We can all envision the wonderful benefits of removing toxic fear, anger, short-term focus, excess accumulation, resource depletion, and relationship imbalances that are initiated by the subject of money and finances in our world. *This global future begins with each of us…impactful individually and powerful community-wide.*

All Roads Lead to Nowhere... or Now-Here?

I've seen this first phrase "All roads lead to nowhere" from time to time referring to the idea that established roads can't really take us to an end destination that we are truly seeking...or that we can never truly "arrive" in fact. Instead, we are usually exhorted to take a road less traveled or, even better, to create our own path as the way to get to a truly meaningful destination and once there achieve further enlightenment.

I would like to offer an additional interpretation with a different focus: "All roads lead to <u>Now-Here.</u>" Each part of our journey, each path that we have taken ~ whether literal or figurative ~ has brought us to where we need to be right here at this moment, fully present, or *now-here*. And the *now-here* is actually the impactful part of the journey – with each authentic, thoughtful component combining with others to create the longer, deeper core of who we are and how we have grown and blossomed.

So, each time you begin or re-read a portion of this book to gain a few more tools to aid in supporting and managing your ongoing financial abundance, please view this as another opportunity to add to the energy and the knowledge that you have already gained throughout your own life. Each step you take and each action you implement is the important part of this experience. There is no set measured accomplishment level you will be rated against or set destination point that will be a human-designated 'you have arrived' award.

Law or Principle?

Perhaps we could really refer to the Law of Attraction instead as the Principle of Attraction.

While reading "The Risen" (2009), August Goforth's book in conversation with his partner Tim Grey, they reminded me that *Laws* are a word we created here in our human form to denote something that solid, unarguable, unchangeable, interminable, indomitable, or however we may want to look at that to get some definition or security in an area. The term *Principle* is more of a guiding idea which opens itself up for further exploration or expansion or discussion – and upon guidance may be modified or adjusted. And one of the main points of this book here is to help us understand that there isn't only one way to approach our financial abundance or spiritual abundance or any other area.

We're each on a very unique and individual journey. And that's why there are so many different options offered here for your consideration, so you can choose those which work for you at a specific time, modify them to your needs, perhaps use something different in the future, or suggest it to someone else who is having some questions or challenges. This becomes more of an evolving process for us rather than once again becoming frustrated and discouraged by trying to do one specific method. Let's take every opportunity to rid ourselves of that old misconceived paradigm of one size fits all, and all those related descriptors and labeling which end up limiting or stopping us right in our tracks.

Financial Decisions Review List

* Own Your Financial Story

* Change Your Financial Story

* Ditch the Limiting Labels

* Count Your Blessings

* Understand Your Needs

* Understand the Cost of Options

* Keep It Simple Sweetie

* Mutual Fair Value

* Priorities and Intentions

* Focus ~ Don't Fuss

* Create Personal Outcomes

* Research, Decide, Move On

* Role Model Service

* Manage Emotional Drivers

* Affirming Communications

* Path of Increasing Finesse

* Thoughtful Planning Mindset

Own Your Financial Story

Buddha is reported to have said, "Truth is bitter in the beginning, sweet in the end, and lies are sweet in the beginning, bitter in the end."

You hold the ultimate creative power for your life, finances included. No one else is responsible at this point: not partners, parents, children, government, financial professionals, bosses, political parties, or other labeled outside sources. Expressions of financial helplessness, denial, or anger divert responsibility, places unreasonable expectations on others, opens blame options, creates health problems, extends dysfunctional behaviors within families and to children, and exacerbates and repeats undesired financial outcomes including lack or cycling abundances.

Reviewing and reconsidering your past experiences and observations is the key to moving forward. We have all had less than ideal situations or information given to us in the past, so you are not alone in your quest to adjust your responses and outlook. To reach our overall goals we have to change our perceptions and intentions, and taking ownership of your financial story redirects the energy and power back to the source who can apply it most fully: <u>yourself.</u>

It's most likely that a good part of what you were taught about money and finances early on in your life came from parents, family members, and teachers who wanted to pass along what they themselves had learned, what had worked for them in the past, and what they thought would help you in the same manner. They may or may not have questioned what they were taught by their own parents and teachers, but their basic intention was to help you succeed as best they understood and to avoid particular problems that they had encountered. So as you continue to have your own internal conversations, bear in mind that in most cases there was no intention to cause you grief or harm later in your own life. You may find that it's helpful and healing to affirm your appreciation for their intentions while being perfectly authentic in moving forward to create your own newly defined path. If there were situations where people intentionally gave you incorrect or harmful information, then the consideration of forgiveness and letting go of anger at the outcomes will have to be part of your own journey.

When we start with the premise that we are here as individual souls on earth to learn from a human experience, then our perspective changes quite a bit. You now have the chance to step back (and up) to view your life from the 10,000 foot level. As a result, the daily details can then be guided by the overarching principles that you choose to embrace.

You also understand that your first goal is to take care of yourself individually and then secondly those people who you most directly support. Thereafter you have additional choices of how you divide your focus further between friends and extended family, charitable contributions and service, building businesses, etc.

No one can give you a magic formula to define or follow an ideal life. For example, who can really say that if you choose the least expensive house or car and you do certain other budget conscious individual steps this makes you a spiritual person on the right track in determining your abundances? Or if you have a larger income, what percentage of donations or contributions is appropriate or acceptable to be viewed as a human on the right spiritual path? It's a matter of conscious perception and intention, and is relative to your unique purposes and goals.

We can have the abundances that we want at very 'visual' different levels. We can be equally happy with a less expensive or more expensive home, car, or wardrobe. The upshot is to learn to be happy and content standing anywhere, anytime, regardless of what you have materially. This personal state then helps us keep perspective about making our choices.

We no longer have to obsess over the best quarter of a rate interest point on investments or on mortgages, or always changing our investments or looking for new hot insurance tools up to the last minute all the time. Certainly, periodic reviews would be helpful so that you make sure that you are paying a reasonable price given changes in offerings and that you still have a tool that works well for your ongoing situation. But is not a game of making changes every week, month, six months or every year.

You can then free up all that energy that you've been using on day-to-day worries to instead help you on your soul's journey with your relationships, with your deeper understandings, and living your authentic life. That's the simple goal of all of these suggestions.

Section Questions:

Who have you given power over your financial choices in the past?

What conversations can you include in your meditation time to consider what is behind your previously accepted expectations or requirements?

How would you like to feel differently about your financial abundance going forward?

Financial Abundance Opening Meditation

- I come to this moment open to new insights, guidance, and ideas

- That will help me personally move into my own unique purposes.

- I agree to acknowledge and experience any challenging thoughts, feelings and emotions that arise now,

- Letting them flow on past - And to understand that I am not the sum of my past fears or experiences.

- I commit to remain open to the universal love and intuition available here,

- And to absorb increasing quantities of that love and trust into myself day by day.

- I come prepared today to actively learn and take my own steps in co-creating the abundance intended for me;

- And I trust that the information and resources I need will be provided through this state of awareness.

- I give thanks for all the many blessings already in my life,

- And am especially grateful for the spirits here now to assist me in my discoveries.

- So Be It.

Change Your Financial Story

*"To live deliberately, you have to think deliberately; and in order to do that, you must have a reference point in order to determine the correction direction of your thought. Right now, just as at the time of your birth, the two necessary factors are in place. The Law of Attraction (the most powerful and consistent Law in the Universe) abounds. And your Guidance System is within you, all queued up and ready to give you directional feedback. You have only one seemingly small but potentially life-changing thing to do: <u>You have to begin telling your story in a new way. You have to tell it as you want it to be.</u>" - **Abraham Hicks***

The greatest gift we have been given is that of free choice…free will to use all the unique and individual experiences and attributes that we have. So we need to accept that along with all the benefits of free will and abundance, there is also our corresponding part in creating what we want. When you continually turn to other people on the outside to give you answers, you will end up unpleasantly surprised or disappointed during some part of the process. From my perspective as a practitioner, the choices must remain in each individual's hands. I cannot in any conscience at all say you must to do this, this, and this ~ and unless you do all these specific things then you're an incomplete person or you are failing somehow.

There are important choices to be made throughout your life, and this relates to being in the moment when making decisions, to making conscious decisions. Going through all the feelings that we have during that process is necessary to really moving forward, instead of continually relying on the myths and masks that I talk about in our financial decisions. We wonder why we don't reach our stated abundances but in many cases we are actually sabotaging out efforts internally. Perhaps we have an inkling deep down that we being our own worst enemy, but we're still going to try to convince ourselves and those around us that we have a really good <u>rational</u> reason why we're doing this.

We need to start with our own financial story and get good at being honest and open with ourselves there first. Otherwise, we can't step up to the plate and teach our children next, and they likely won't understand how to make good financial choices on their own. Or we won't learn to say no to a family member or friend who is unable to handle a personal loan and we don't help them understand other options - so they become dependent on us and we become upset that they haven't paid us back. Or we verbalize that we're too busy with our schedules and we can't take care of our own financial health, when in effect if we took an hour every day and focused on ourselves, not only would our health improve (because we are mind/body/spirit), but then our ability for care for others would effectively expand exponentially.

When we step back and take a look at our choices we can really receive that wonderful gift of free will that we've been given, and that ties into our whole perception, intentions, and the way that we make choices. And making conscious, thoughtful choices the best we can at any given point in time is really the key. That's how we really learn in relationships, our own endeavors, in our own creations, and our own explorations. If we deprive ourselves of that opportunity to exercise free will, we're really depriving ourselves of all the chances to learn and grow.

We go through just as many emotions, feelings, and consequences when rushing through these financial decisions as we do when we rush through relationship decisions and choices. And in fact, since in our culture money ties into everything, if we aren't able to face making financial decisions prudently, that has an impact on everything else: our health, who we choose as partners, how we treat our family members, how we can raise and influence our children, and how can we participate in the community. So dealing with the finances and being present in the moment there is just as important as having a well thought out list of who you want to have as your marriage partner or your business partner. We tend to skip over that conscious choice process with finances because we figure that's something external when actually it's very much a part of our manifestation.

Section Questions:

What new financial outcomes do you want to incorporate into your life, and why?

How do you feel your health, relationships, work purpose, or other areas will change or improve with these new outcomes?

How can you take back your own power and initiative to change your personal financial story?

Ditch the Limiting Labels

A large part of increasing our vibrational status is found in expanding our energy flows and the radius of our personal energy space. We serve many in many roles during our earthly lives, so there's no beneficial reason to pigeon-hole or condense ourselves into a handful of labels or positions. When we resolutely stick to standard phrases or explanations of who we are or why we respond in certain ways, we reinforce our own internal limitations and do ourselves in. The outside influences we usually blame really aren't a driving factor in comparison to our own constraints.

My first book "Financial Stewardship," Chapter Three, contained three pages of common statements or posturing I've heard over the years from people of all ages. A few of the top comments are:

- ❋ Financial planning is all about investments and making the best return, and since I don't have any money to invest I don't need to do any planning.

- ❋ I often say to others that I'm clueless about financial matters and preface my questions with words like 'dumb, silly, and stupid'.

- ❋ I was never good at math so I'll never understand money, taxes, and all the economic talk.

- ❋ I care about teaching, healing, the arts, the environment, and other service activities...so I have no time or interest in money or management.

- My partner handles all our financial stuff and says he or she has everything under control, so there's no need for me to get into those matters.

- Looking at my budget and bank account make me nervous and upset, so I just ignore that as long as possible so I don't feel bad.

- Things are really tough, but God/the Universe will provide if I have enough faith and turn it all over to him/them to handle.

- I just simply hate money and talking about it, and would be really happy in my life if I didn't have to deal with it.

- Money is a bad driver in our economy…just look at all the greed, stealing, lying, and other behavior that goes along with it.

These statements on the surface may appear to emotionally remove the individual from the topic of money or distance themselves from the effects of being involved. However, I and my other practicing colleagues sense deeply how much fear, denial, uncertainty, anxiety, and feelings of helplessness still actually remain under the cover of these 'reasonings.' And trying to bury these emotions just adds more layers of negative vibrations and clogged energy flows year by year.

There are many interesting books and commentaries on 'archetypes' ~ prime examples, paradigms, or patterns identified by the authors to categorize and explain certain types of observed, repeated human behaviors. The often used personality tests also involve extensive questions to try to more easily identify and quantify certain descriptors for use in career or job placements. I certainly believe that using a variety of resources to learn more about ourselves through internal review and assessment can increase our awareness levels and provide some new insights and open areas for self-development (i.e., astrology, metaphysical treatises, behavioral models, etc.) In the past I've used a number of offerings from various authors and researchers myself, and it can be very positive to tap into their respective studies to expand my own horizons as well.

That said, though, I've also discovered that it can be pretty tempting to begin to rely on others' assessments of who you are, what categories you represent, how it's predicted you will respond in certain situations, and what your anticipated future outcomes will be. After all, these are published, credentialed, recognized experts in this field and how could an individual experience possibly stack up to all this data, the well written explanations, and the neatly presented labels?

The archetype/personality/behavioral models that are presented by conscientious authors do come with the caveat that each particular myth or story is just a current starting point to better understand an individual's present manifestation. And those writers do counsel readers to do some internal questioning to find better balance and contemplate more productive behaviors when applicable. However, if you were to find yourself labeled as a 'caregiver/empath' type, for example in a particular text, there's a tendency to say to yourself and others, "That's how I'm wired...I just have to look out for other people and it is just part of my experience to be on the short end of receiving. If my health or own life suffers otherwise, well that's what my life is supposed to be." Or perhaps you find a 'warrior/rescuer' category fits your current traits, so you feel compelled to continue trying to fix the world's problems by charging into situations convinced that you have, or must find, the right answers and let everyone else know what they should be doing. Or maybe you select two or three models that seem to fit you in the present and you alternate back and forth between explanations of how you are supposed to respond and react. The same traps potentially apply with generalized assumptions related to astrology signs, numerology, choosing static totems or physical representations, cultural titles, past life stories, and more.

I want to strongly encourage you to take such information about all personal tendencies and skills with *several grains of salt* for two important reasons. One, we have been given the abilities and divine assistance necessary to modify our current lives and create new stories for ourselves based on consciously defined intentions and priorities. Second, I believe there is also a missing link in the usually accepted archetype/ myth process that critically skews our perception of our present 'reality.'

By the time in our lives where we are taking personality tests or reading books about archetypes and history myths, we are of an age that we've spent sufficient time on earth being greatly impacted by parents, institutions, religious teachings, friends, workplace expectations, and many other cultural influences. We have moved further and further away from our actual physical birth date and the initial time where we came with our truly original purpose and knowledge. We lose track of many of our intended traits and innate wisdoms; instead these qualities have been submerged in favor of the responses we learned in order to actually survive in our particular physical life.

So the labels that we are measured against within these tests and charts are, in significant part, ones we've been taught and reinforced while on planet Earth - not purely our intrinsic, intended qualities. To get back to our complete authentic purposes, we have to explore even further beyond these archetypal references and titles. Choosing or modifying a different archetype or myth story, or even combining a few, doesn't take us far enough back in our quest. *And this is where your own individual story experience can indeed trump all the credentialed, professional, published information in this world.*

The scope of how to begin or continue with these personal explorations and re-writing your personal contract is far beyond the function of this book. Readings and professional resources in the realms of shamanism, intuitive readings, past life regressions, hypnosis, psychotherapy counseling, neuro-linguistic programming, personal meditations, spiritual retreats and discussions, and other authentic coaches may be helpful options to you depending upon your interests and intentions. The vital message of this section is to raise your awareness of your capability and power to change your personal story – financial and otherwise.

You don't need to choose yet another pre-defined role to emulate. Discover and design your own unique role and costumes!

Section Questions:

What personal labels have you been using in your financial life to describe yourself or your financial experiences?

Where and when did you acquire these labels and explanations (from family, friends, media, religious teachings, etc.)?

What other descriptors (archetype, personality test, family viewpoints, etc.) have you absorbed and been using in your decision-making processes?

How have they been limiting your energy levels and abilities to envision different financial outcomes?

Count Your Blessings

Yes, this old adage can really be even more effective than you ever imagined before. Start every day with a very specific listing of the blessings and comforts in your life – not just a general 'thanks for everything' tossed out as you race toward the front door. I guarantee there will be a major shift in your vibrations as you truly realize each time that you could go on and on about the wonderful people, abilities, and comforts you *already* have in your life: sight, breath, smell, arms and legs, hearing, pets, bed, water, trees, light, each friend/colleague/family member, movement, grass, sun, food, vehicle, home, town services, clothing, clouds, flowers, heat, medical assistance…you get the picture that's rapidly developing here.

A friend of mine shared with me that when she chooses to find small ways to show her gratitude for the blessings she has, whether volunteering periodically or contributing to an offering plate (even one dollar per week during a period when she was unemployed) she regularly notices even greater abundances coming back to her: a $50 check from a relative with a note saying they were thinking of her and to use the enclosed for something helpful, or a suggestion from a friend about a new job opening, or a contractor friend finding a simple, cost effective way to take care of an unexpected but necessary household repair.

When we really recognize what we already have for abundance, the anxiety-produced pressure to 'get this NOW' or 'I NEED this' flows away and is replaced by more thoughtful priorities and considered choices. If there is something you would LIKE to add to your life, that's wonderful and perfectly fine to put out that request and adapt your own energies to move in that direction. However, if we stay stuck in a habitual swirl of pressure to get something new right away, to either fill a longing, take up time in our schedules, or engage a sense of temporary comfort, then we end up making decisions for unhealthy reasons and selections that are out of sync with our real purposes. It's the same analogy used to help us successfully change eating habits and make different health choices: learn to make increasing steps of mindful choices that generate new rewards for your authentic self.

Abundance is state of perception – a place of being - not a dollar amount or lifestyle The more you feel you already have in your life, the less you will desire new items or feel a need to have the newest version of an item 'just because'. You will be better able to recognize the priority areas in your life and find appropriate items to invest in, and will bypass fads or substitutions. For example, before you go shopping for an item reflect on the riches you already have in your home. Consider if you have an existing item that could be repurposed to meet this desire or what you might relinquish to make space for a new object. Consider how much you can actually afford to spend at the moment, not just what price is marketed to you as a great deal. If acquiring this item would create harm elsewhere in your life (i.e. unpaid bills, increasing credit extensively, lying to your partner, post-purchase stress and second guessing, etc.) then that's a pretty clear sign to take some time out and rethink your actions.

If your budget is sufficient to purchase this item without undue stress, think about whether it will support your considered goals and purposes. For example, buying new clothing could be a very reasonable action, unless you are doing so in an attempt to please someone else with a particular piece of apparel or you have similar items in your closet that still bear tags and never provided service after being the last 'must have.' As another example, if you are considering buying a particular new home, articulate if and how this change will allow you to add further to your life purpose, perhaps having/adopting/fostering children, holding charity events, providing a regular gathering place for family, space for a new business venture, personal peace and quiet space for learning, etc. Or do you find yourself simply repeating phrases from television or friends or co-workers such as 'you deserve a dream home' or 'this will show I've arrived' or 'I'm supposed to buy a house to be an adult' or 'I need to buy this now because mortgage rates are so good.'

As I mentioned before, there's nothing incorrect or unhealthy about using money to purchase items or enjoy earthly experiences. We are offered many different types of abundances here and when we receive them openly it is a wonderful outcome for everyone. The balance line is why and how we make our choices. Each of us has the power to manifest new outcomes and that power will be channeled one way or another. Let's take a bit of time to feel the true bottom line motivator: fear, anger, security…or heart purpose, expansion, and happiness?

Think about how you will feel during the days following a purchase. Will you joyfully include this item on your list of daily blessings? Or will you have a niggling feeling that you could have made a more meaningful and relaxed choice if you had been coming from a more grounded, grateful state of being?

Financial Abundance Opening Meditation

- I come to this moment open to new insights, guidance, and ideas

- That will help me personally move into my own unique purposes.

- I agree to acknowledge and experience any challenging thoughts, feelings and emotions that arise now,

- Letting them flow on past - And to understand that I am not the sum of my past fears or experiences.

- I commit to remain open to the universal love and intuition available here,

- And to absorb increasing quantities of that love and trust into myself day by day.

- I come prepared today to actively learn and take my own steps in co-creating the abundance intended for me;

- And I trust that the information and resources I need will be provided through this state of awareness.

- I give thanks for all the many blessings already in my life,

- And am especially grateful for the spirits here now to assist me in my discoveries.

- So Be It.

Understand Your Needs

Abraham Hicks offers a wonderful exercise envisioning that each day you receive an increasingly larger monetary deposit into your checking account, and then you *figuratively* spend those dollars over and over to reinforce the sensation of freedom and endless possibilities when you begin to remove the external perception and influence of a less than desired current financial abundance state. This is an excellent tool to help shift both your short and long term vibrations and will go a long way to manifesting your new goals. However, many people end up inadvertently sabotaging this exercise because on a daily basis they *literally* end up spending their currently earned income multiple times over by avoiding current stewardship principles of planning and following their resources.

Whether you earn $20,000 or $1 million each year, you need to have a basic spending and savings plan in place in order to make informed decisions about your finances. There's just no way around really knowing your current financial position and understanding what you can accomplish with your current earnings.

If you don't know how you are presently using the resources you have been given, it will not be possible to make beneficial adjustments or to determine how to clearly express new preferences to manifest. And if you have not yet built the skill set necessary to effectively manage what you currently receive, how could you have the strength and discernment to fully manage even more resources?

Most people have constructed such an aversion in their minds to planning that they now believe a budget:

1) is a four-letter word,

2) will take a great deal of time to pull together, and

3) will forever doom them to rules, limitations, and anxiety.

I'm here to share with you that the actual outcome is exactly opposite of those three presumptions:

1) Getting a handle on your cash flow each month/year will be one of the best gifts you can ever give yourself;

2) Depending on the complexity of your lifestyle, the current basic numbers can be recorded within 10-30 minutes;

3) Writing down actual figures removes the mind's unsustainable attempt to juggle categories and rationalize old habits on a piecemeal basis; and

4) Facing the full picture all at once will dispel the denial, procrastination, and invented fears and replace them instead with black and white information, clarity about current choices, and enlightenment about new possibilities.

So what happens to your vibrational levels when you are being proactive, making conscious choices, and more clearly understanding what you want to co-create? I can tell you from thousands of personal and client experiences that you shift several vibrational levels upward and you open so many new doors that you had previously locked on yourself.

Consider the idea that preparing your spending and saving plan is really an additional component to the other journaling insights that you record and review in a written word format. When you really look at your calendar and your checkbook (or online bank records), it becomes pretty clear how you are spending your time and your resources. If you don't like some of what you see, then you can adjust accordingly and take a new review periodically to verify you really are matching your actions with your words. And having such basic information as how your income and expenses tie into your internal wishes will be a major factor in being able to move yourself toward specific changes – not to mention having more relevant conversations with the universe about how you all can work together cooperatively for your highest and best good.

Please note that going through this spending plan exercise can also be a healthy eye-opener for those of you who have accumulated truly sufficient resources but are still feeling reluctant to spend money on yourself or share with others because of an ingrained (but unsubstantiated) fear of running out of funds, feeling undeserving of receiving abundance, or experiencing other related blocks which have not yet been addressed.

So what are your options for setting down a basic monthly or annual outline of your current income and expenses? First, if you prefer working with a tangible piece of paper, then you can assemble a blank page, pencil and a calculator.

Create an outline that includes a listing of your income items such as: salary paycheck, social security, interest income, retirement account distribution, pension, part time job earnings, business income, and other. Put the dollar amounts in a column next to the description. Now, same process for expenses such as: mortgage/rent, cell phone, internet, electric, heating gas/propane, water, vehicle loan/lease, auto gas, food, healthcare, books, education, charitable contributions, hobbies/activities, pet care, clothing, child care/camps, insurances (auto, home, life, umbrella, long term care, etc.), dining out, entertainment, travel, personal care, property taxes if not included in the mortgage figure, income taxes, savings contribution, *and (yes!) a miscellaneous/blow it line* – a little mental flexibility goes a long way in staying on track for the big picture.

Take a few minutes to think about your daily and weekly routines to see what other categories you may have overlooked initially and need to include for a full picture. And do be honest about how much you spend at the grocery store or how often you go out for meals and entertainment. These are two areas in particular that people tend to underestimate dramatically. If you are really not sure what the totals will be, start saving your store receipts and bank withdrawal slips for a few weeks and then double check those again. You can use 'rounded numbers' such as to the nearest $10 or $50 or $100 to make addition and analysis easier. Add up the expense items and subtract them from the income figures. The net amount will quickly show you where you stand in your stewardship computation.

Second, when you can work with an Excel worksheet (or similar program), it will be fairly easy to create a couple of different sheets to experiment with reallocating funds within various expense categories – and the computations are done for you automatically (although you should do a quick reality check or manual computation anyway initially to make sure there isn't a flaw in equations somewhere.) Unless you are quite keen to create a custom spreadsheet for yourself, there are some simple templates available that you can save under different names for your own use – such as those found when selecting a personal budget template as a new document. Use the standard template to start and either delete categories you aren't currently using or add in ones specific to your own life. Save often to make sure new information inputs aren't wiped out in error. You can also create various 'test' or 'projection' plans to help you more clearly see the affect and interaction of new ideas you may have for allocating current or future resources.

Third, you can schedule an appointment with your CPA or Certified Financial Planner to have some assistance in fully completing the categories and, even more importantly, to help you more objectively and less stressfully analyze the information while talking through options and professional suggestions. These advisers can provide a real coaching role to get you moving in the new directions you seek, and their interactions with hundreds and thousands of clients give you access to information and options you may not have tapped in your own sphere of resources. Talking with someone else about both your income/expenses and the assets you have accumulated offers you a sounding board to keep your authentic wishes and priorities front and center. *As always, you are the creator of your future and therefore hold the decision-making calls.* It is beneficial sometimes, though, to have a supportive resource to boost your energy levels and affirm your abilities during important transition times. Many financial educators and coaches offer appointment flexibility ranging from a one-time session on a specific topic to multiple phases for a comprehensive review.

As you look at the bottom line of your figures, there are some common questions and thoughts that arise. You are not alone in wondering if you're making good decisions for yourself or whether there are other options available that you aren't aware of or didn't think would work in your own situation. I'd like to share a few of these specific examples so you get a real sense that you are connected with many others in this awareness-building. In addition, you'll learn that there are some very concrete ways to adjust your current scenario to generate the different outcomes that really speak to your purpose. Please keep in mind through all the examples that what works for one person or family may not be appropriate for another – so comparing notes with friends or asking a professional for 'percentage guidelines' will not give you a universal seal of approval or confirmation.

1) You may realize that you are spending a lot more in certain categories than you really thought. If these are discretionary items, such as dining out or entertainment outings, then you can pretty quickly decide whether or not to continue doing so. You may choose to continue these activities and understand now why you don't have as much money left over at the end of the month as you would have previously thought. Or you may feel that you would rather reallocate some of that spending to another area – whether that's savings, travel trips, or gifts. Adjusting your lifestyle in terms of housing, work-related expenses, or other big ticket items may also be considered.

2) Another outcome may be that you have identified some areas that are causing you to go into debt regularly because your income and expenses don't match. You can either then consciously choose to address that issue of credit use or this may trigger some personal discussions about whether you are being compensated appropriately in your work given your skills, expertise, and contributions. If you are being paid equitably within your company or industry, then taking some time to re-match your current resources is necessary, or you may choose to investigate another position or field that can provide economically for the lifestyle that is important to you.

3) You may conclude from the information that expense items that were once of great importance to you are no longer tied into new goals and desires that have developed. You may also realize that you want to add a new category – so then consider how allocating resources to that new item impacts the rest of your financial commitments.

4) You might see that you are actually receiving sufficient financial abundance from your income sources but that you haven't been tracking or using it as efficiently or effectively as otherwise possible. By making future decisions from this place of new awareness you can now adjust certain categories to create even more long term benefits for yourself, your family, or your global focus.

5) When you have a solid summary of your current financial resources in hand, you can then move on to the stage of envisioning different future options – and you now have a better feel for the interactions of your choices. Doing 'projections' (testing out varying combinations of income and spending) gives you a visual way to see what issues you may want to address to reach those scenarios (different lifestyle, different career, different physical location, etc.) *Having a physical, visual tool in hand*

removes the mind-consuming, power-draining swirl of figures, what if's, and unknown consequences of your daily financial thoughts and worries.

When beginning this process of understanding your needs, it's not uncommon to feel like you're just opening a whole can of proverbial worms and you're not sure how to handle them well. I want to reassure you that when you take this first step, the seemingly problematic worms will soon become butterflies with some thoughtful nurturing and expectation. There may well be some uncomfortable moments working through resistance and asking about options. But those will be passing in nature as you commit to honesty, communication, and new opportunities.

Section Questions:

What did I discover about my own current financial state by doing this budget exercise?

What changes and new outcomes can I now work towards with this new information?

How does looking at various options (projections) expand my thinking about future possibilities and choices?

Understand the Cost of Options

Hand in hand with understanding your needs and wishes is the critical point of understanding all the costs of the options you are considering in terms of money, time, short and long term trade-offs, implications on your value principles, consistency in your personal integrity, and the effect on others around you. Our decisions and choices do not exist in a vacuum, and they do indeed have a vibrational impact for us going forward as well. Remember that both not making a decision and ignoring a situation are in fact choices on your part. There are always options available to us even though we may sometimes try to convince ourselves otherwise, perhaps out of a misguided wish to just 'do something' or a reluctance to allocate some thoughtful time in an already booked daily schedule.

I meet many people each week who are making plans for very large purchases or investments involving tens of thousands or hundreds of thousands of dollars (such as buying a home, starting a business, signing for college loans, participating in a hot new investment opportunity, moving cross country for a 'better life', etc.) yet they think they are being 'financially savvy' by not allocating some dollars and a few hours of their time to get professional consultation in advance. When I listen to folks talk about problems they encountered in such endeavors or how deals didn't work out as they had hoped, they appear so surprised to hear that they actually had other options, alternatives and combinations of solutions that would have eliminated or minimized the downsides they experienced.

As a culture we provide very little in the way of true financial education programs that encourage understanding, critical thinking, and personal decision-making. Yet we somehow have convinced ourselves that we need to *sound* very experienced in the financial realm and express the relevant answers for each situation even though we've never been through it personally or spent any time doing true homework in preparation. Once we've made a decision, we often feel compelled to doggedly stick with it, regardless of how a situation is developing or new information that becomes available meriting consideration. When we take a step back and open up to a more flexible view, however, we can much better understand (and feel) that there are very few absolutely right or must do responses; instead we can focus on what matters to our own plan for our own purposes for our own timing. And knowing the various trade-offs involved in our decisions helps us make informed choices that are consistent with both our short and long term goals and intentions.

Please keep in mind that there are many financial education professionals available around the country who have dedicated themselves to the high standards of their credentials, continual learning, and personal service. They are in a good place to provide objective, non-agenda based ideas to help you create your own custom choices with thoughtful use of your resources. The return on investment (ROI) that you will receive from interacting with these individuals will *far exceed* the usual stock market ROI that is bandied about regularly as the key measurement of financial prowess.

As an example, during a recent Financial Literacy workshop I offered, a participant expressed frustration that she felt the colleges and banks were conspiring against hardworking parents by making them take out large student loans at varying interest rates in order to achieve the goal of higher educational opportunities for their children. She is presently quite stressed and strapped about the repayment of loans and felt that when the paperwork was presented to the family that it was a 'take it or leave it' deal on the table. Without some advance preparation in place, she had been completely governed by fear and anxiety at those moments, and so wasn't able to be aware at the time that she really did have other personally empowering options, such as renegotiate with the school about the combination of grants/work study/scholarships/loans, have a family discussion that such a loan amount was not a prudent amount for them to manage but perhaps "x" amount was reasonable, look at other potential schools, learn about other types of loans or funding alternatives, or engage a professional college/financial advisor for assistance.

Many grandparents, relatives, or godparents have also felt compelled to co-sign student loans for beloved students without having separate financial advisement, and the results have been quite devastating for older adults who then had a significant repayment burden to be faced on fixed or decreasing incomes themselves.

Whether it's for student loans, vehicle or home purchases, special activities programs, or other large commitments, making quick decisions while feeling under pressure without benefit of considering your true priorities, financial abilities and options, and possible ramifications will impact your freedom and flexibility. Future plans and wishes may be detoured, and hard lessons incurred that will take a longer period of time and the application of more energy to get back to where you originally hoped to be.

Please note, however, that I've used the term 'detoured' deliberately here to also indicate that it is always possible to reset your path, as we do with our GPS systems, to reach your ultimate desired destination. *Using new resources and investigating adjustments can deliver very different results for you even after a less than desirable selection.* You will need to take action to do so, and not succumb to the emotion of defeat or apathy for any length of time. Taking the time to make current choices or adjustments that preserve or raise your growing energy and positive vibrations keeps you moving along the abundance path in all areas of life.

Section Questions:

Has there been a past financial situation where I've/we've made a quick decision that did not take all consequences into consideration? If so, what lessons can be learned that will help me going forward?

If you have a current situation to address, what factors can you identify now that may affect how you make a choice right now (i.e., long-term budget impact, effect on partners, cost of item versus the value of my time, etc.)?

What resources beyond your current experience and knowledge can you tap into to better understand and appreciate how to identify your options?

Keep It Simple Sweetie

A colleague of mine reminded me that this process of growing on our journey is supposed to be en-<u>lighten</u>-ment, not *en-<u>heavy</u>-ment*. So when you find you're getting frustrated with yourself or being less than compassionate with your efforts (as we all do at various times), then that's definitely the moment to consciously step back from your overly-dedicated pursuits and return to the simple basics again.

Simple does not equate to simplistic, which is defined in thesaurus.com as 'condensed, overly or misleadingly simplified.' Simple also does not refer to reducing a situation to a black/white or positive/negative label, but rather actually supports a return to the primary priorities and goals for what you want to achieve and what options will support those purposes.

In the financial arena there are thousands of financial tools out there available to address a thousand different situations. *The first and most important question for you is to determine what <u>you</u> really need to support <u>your</u> primary goals. A plan or solution that works very well for one person may create a complete mess for someone else.* Boil down both your needs and the product impacts to the basics and don't get caught up in industry terminology or marketing tactics. If the particular advisor or resource cannot explain directly and clearly to you what a product impact will be now and in the future for your <u>entire</u> financial picture, then find another one who either has more expertise or a more compatible communication style. Written product information and summaries should also be clear, transparent for cost and benefit, and provided for your review prior to any signed commitments on your part.

For example, as you've been reviewing your overall financial picture, you have an inclination to research whether a life insurance policy of some type could be a part of your financial plan to achieve goals of providing resources for loved ones or making a charitable bequest. Before you begin reading too much online information or speaking with a licensed insurance advisor, you first think about why you believe you need to have extra resources available through such a policy and what benefits you would like to cover in terms of considering a total policy value. You also understand your current income and expenses, so determining a prudent spending amount for the policy is possible and fairly quick to assess. You review your initial stated goal to understand whether you are coming from a place of anxiety, fear, marketing pressure, cultural assumptions, or a genuine balanced place of considering available product tools.

If you determine that a specific policy amount would provide your loved ones with a financial cushion to tide them over during an adjustment period after your passing and your budget allows for a modest monthly premium, then your research would focus on a term life insurance offering – which provides straightforward coverage on an annual basis (similar to your auto or homeowners insurance) and can be renewed each year. You would not need to get into complexities of universal life, whole life, or combination products that require a much larger premium payment and may have investment-related components included as well. Although an experienced insurance advisor will likely have additional truly helpful insights into current products and other viable options to think about, the approach of conveying your needs and thought-process to the advisor helps keep the overall focus on your personal goals and minimizes the chances that the conversation could quickly devolve into a potentially confusing, frustrating, off-target discussion. The same process would also hold true if you are coming from a place of needing a more sophisticated planning solution – and the resulting actions steps would be appropriate for you given the legitimately different goals and resources.

If you really don't understand the terms of a product or how exactly it will impact your life, then you should not proceed with that particular implementation at that time. However, it's vital that you step up to the plate mentally and emotionally to learn about, focus on, and truly consider the information available to you. Falling back into personal statements such as "I've never been good at this stuff before" or "It sounds complicated so I'll just defer to my partner or ignore this completely" lands squarely into the lower vibrational responses and only reinforces your perceived lack of personal power and choice. Denial, procrastination, and abdication of responsibility are insidious growers of fear, worry, stress, and anger - and those states of mind are contrary to manifesting expansion and abundances.

On the flip side, when you reach out and truly seek to make choices that align with your core priorities, you feel a wonderful relief sensation that affirms your overall missions and lifts your energy up and forward. Adding up all the individual decisions in this way is what keeps our journey moving in the direction that brings us relaxation, fulfillment, and enlightenment. This process is situationally unconditional, removes us from the supposedly well-intentioned warning of 'Be careful about feeling too good as the other shoe may drop,' and contributes to a stronger foundation for future decisions.

Contrary to much cultural hype we hear, telling a simpler story is not a less rewarding or less meaningful story; it is truly the most authentic, aware, and impactful story we have to experience and share.

Section Questions:

Are there certain financial situations where I usually put off addressing an issue because I'm worried everything will feel overwhelming or complicated?

What tools can I use to help me readjust my concerns and take a more active role in defining my primary goals?

If a decision process seems to be getting more complicated or confusing over time, how can I re-direct or re-state my overarching intentions to return to a simpler, more effective outcome?

Mutual Fair Value

Simply stated: Value your own time and resources appropriately and value the time and resources of others accordingly.

Unless you are in a mutually recognized situation (garage sale, flea market, auction, etc.) financial savvy does not mean haggling or expecting discounts. Would you accept an employer reducing your paycheck every week by x% because they felt they were having a tough week and deserved a break or just weren't in the mood to shell out 'that much' money? Or how would you feel if a consulting client withheld part of your fee at the end of a project because they believed in hindsight that they could have done the job less expensively themselves?

Those professionals who understand their own value and are proficient in their expertise do not offer significant 'free' services – perhaps some introductory materials, a short consult, or a special charitable contribution from time to time. However, they do not present themselves as begging for attention at all costs or trying to force client interactions that are not appropriate at a given time. A quality mechanic would not offer to fix your car for free just to prove their worth to you specifically – nor would they presume to provide a recommendation without running diagnostics to customize your vehicles repair. A nutritionist would not buy your groceries, or a hair stylist give you free cuts for a three-month trial. And you would not provide such services to your employer or business clients. So we can thoughtfully and firmly step away from the cultural expectation that economic transactions should be a win-lose proposition.

Please remember that ALL types of work can be done in such a way as to be of service to fellow human beings, whether as a maintenance caretaker, doctor, teacher, counselor, artist, financial practitioner, attorney, animal caretaker, environmental steward, public safety professional, craftsman, spiritual healer, and every other combination. Everyone can truly be a 'service industry' contributing in their own unique ways.

Blindly or passively/aggressively accepting less than adequate remuneration for your particular vocation is not an authentic affirmation of your own true value. And, conversely, paying less than appropriate value for a high-quality service under the guise of presuming that the provider receives sufficient other psychic rewards (public recognition, brownie points toward 'heaven', ego boosts, the thrill of sales competition, or other similar connotations) is simply a shadowed means of not respecting another's contributions.

When it comes to purchasing products, whether that is a house, piece of furniture, article of clothing, insurance policies, or anything else you could envision, there is no such thing as free shipping, free financing, or no fees. A business must charge a price that covers all its expenses in order to stay in operation, so the shipping company must be paid to deliver an item to your doorstep, that company has to earn interest on the funds they are loaning you, and an agent/representative needs to be paid out of the product cost.

It's truly just a shell game of marketing terms to view otherwise…an attempt to manipulate the belief of the consumer somehow pulling off a really unique deal or the provider magically offering a quality 'something' for nothing in monetary terms. Take a few moments to reflect on the terms in a purchase situation and consider whether you feel comfortable that the exchange is truly a mutual value focus.

Section Questions:

Are there times when I've sold myself short on my financial contributions value and worth? Why did these situations occur?

Are there particular times when I feel compelled to focus on getting a good deal financially without considering the transaction impact on the other party?

What would be some healthy reasons to shift my views on the value of my own time and money?

How can I create win-win transactions for services and goods for both myself and providers?

Financial Abundance Opening Meditation

* I come to this moment open to new insights, guidance, and ideas

* That will help me personally move into my own unique purposes.

* I agree to acknowledge and experience any challenging thoughts, feelings and emotions that arise now,

* Letting them flow on past - And to understand that I am not the sum of my past fears or experiences.

* I commit to remain open to the universal love and intuition available here,

* And to absorb increasing quantities of that love and trust into myself day by day.

* I come prepared today to actively learn and take my own steps in co-creating the abundance intended for me;

* And I trust that the information and resources I need will be provide

* I give thanks for all the many blessings already in my life,

* And am especially grateful for the spirits here now to assist me in my discoveries.

* So Be It.

Priorities and Intentions

The key to effectively and consistently making financial choices that truly support your purpose is to *choose your life goals first and align money decisions second.* Once you determine your priorities and intentions there are many options to support and accomplish your desired results. Keeping the focus on your most important life criteria generates great benefits, including less confusion, not getting bogged down in extraneous details, eliminating regular bouts of analysis paralysis, remaining on-track with your plans to manifest chosen outcomes, and much easier implementation of necessary changes in your habits and behaviors.

As you place your attention on the positive rewards of your chosen priorities and intentions, your energy vibrations shift to higher, more pleasant and productive levels. Your thoughts and emotions now have a tangible target to consider, and you have much smoother, synchronistic flows with your actions steps.

For a familiar introductory example, consider how you would feel differently about these two situations regarding your physical health:

First scenario: You decide to start an exercise program because you think you should meet the parameters of a chart for height/weight/body fat you've seen in some recent health magazines. You're determined to lose the weight as quickly as possible so you also decide to eliminate carbs, chocolate, and snacks at the same time. It's annoying that you also have a lot of other 'To Do's" to handle at the moment, but hey, that's life, right?

Pretty soon you're beating yourself up because you missed a couple of days of jogging and you're really cranky because you feel deprived of all treats and comfort food. Plus, it's getting tiresome trying to measure out the food and get the recommended mix of nutrients. After a few weeks of this on-again, off-again activity, it appears your efforts to get to a desired numerical weight figure are taking you even further away from those results. You're tired of having to force yourself into a new routine of exercise, overwhelmed with the details of the new food regime, and angry with yourself for not being disciplined enough. You throw in the proverbial towel and decide you'll try again when you find the right program that will provide quicker results.

Second scenario: You decide you want to have more physical energy to do more fun activities with your kids/grandkids/nieces/nephews/younger friends. These activities will help you spend more time together and create lasting bonds and memories. During the first week you dust off your old bicycle, inflate the tires, and go explore a local bike trail on the days it's not raining. Some days you don't feel like getting on the bike, but walking for a while is a good option too. You plan an active outing day with the kids for an upcoming Saturday about three weeks out, and thinking about this reward keeps you doing some kind of exercise every day. You feel good about the new steps you're taking so it's pretty easy to serve yourself some slightly smaller portions of your favorite foods most days. Even when two special parties come up that provide extra tempting food, you sample everything that looks good but decide not to go back for seconds. When the Saturday activity event arrives, your pants are fitting a bit better, you participate in all but one of the day's activities, and the kids are asking, "When can we do this again?"

In the second scenario, you chose a priority, intention, and an accompanying reward that really excited you and tapped your natural energy and authentic interests. You're able to make these incremental choices because you have a personal vision of a healthier you having a great time at the upcoming events and enjoying them more than ever. And you've left open the door to additional options that can help you even further along with your goals: planning new menus, trying some new local foods from the farmers' market, joining a walking group, etc. You also choose to focus on this one main area of change during that month, giving yourself time to develop some new habits and behaviors that are now becoming second nature.

───

It can seem rather daunting to launch significant changes in your life, so I offer the following exercise developed for a client workshop that you can experiment with and adjust to make your own. *Especially when you're starting out with this new approach, if you become aware you're trying to make choices that don't relate to top 3 priorities you identified, then set aside those decisions for the time being until you can better focus. This particular step will help minimize the chance that you will feel overwhelmed and make contradictory or conflicting choices from a financial standpoint.*

Match Your Spiritual Intentions
and Your Financial Resolutions
©Changing Times Planning, 2015

Beginning Exercise: Choose <u>any three words</u> from the list below that hold particular meaning for you at this time ~ then list them in order of current priority. Write yourself a note as to why each concept is important to you (intention), what your goal/reward would be for moving toward each vision, and what you think are related financial considerations.

(Variations: add your own words of particular meaning, select up to 5 words, use annually as a 'check-up' or as needed when experiencing changing situations, do this exercise with your partner, family, or friends)

Security	Options	Flexibility
Health	Family	Partnership
Creativity	New Venture	Home
Education	Learning	Career
Relationship	Relaxation	Energy
Mission	Outreach	Travel
Organization	Action	Enjoyment
Planning	Preparation	Legacy

Priority

_____   _____   _____

Intentions

_____   _____   _____

_____   _____   _____

Goal/Reward

_____   _____   _____

_____   _____   _____

Financial Considerations

_____   _____   _____

_____   _____   _____

_____   _____   _____

Additional Notes:

Example 1

Priority: Health

Intention: Better honor my body and its contributions

Goal/Reward: More energy, stamina, service; less illness

Financial Considerations: Let family know I would appreciate birthday/holiday monies toward a bicycle instead of clothing store gift cards, set aside consultation fee with health professional for personal suggestions, adjust my budget categories to focus on appropriate spending habits for better food

Example 2

Priority: Education

Intention: Prepare myself for new career purpose

Goal/Reward: More personal satisfaction, work aligned better with my interests and purpose, less daily harmful stress

Financial Considerations: Identify cost effective and flexible learning options, save and allocate money for professional certificate or educational programs, plan my transition budget between current and new careers

Example 3

Priority: Relationships

Intention: Develop deeper meaningful ties with my family

Goal/Reward: Less family friction and stress, better understanding of everyone's needs, more family fun time and experiences

Financial Considerations: Schedule consultation(s) with communication coach/counselor to begin new skills, allocate special funds for regular family events and activities instead of extra new household items, shift or reduce extra work hours to gain some family time

Example 4

Priority: Security

Intention: Make plans for a stronger financial situation

Goal/Reward: Feel less anxious each day, be more excited about my future, be part of fun and rewarding activities and events

Financial Considerations: Understand my current and future spending needs, align my income and savings with those needs, focus (and spend) on only those items and people that support my long-term goals, research new options to create my desired lifestyle

Section Questions:

Were you surprised by particular feelings that came up when choosing your initial priority words?

How do you see all your listed priorities tying together to create the life you want?

What benefits will you personally experience by now choosing life goals first and then aligning your financial decisions accordingly?

What differences in priorities came up when you did this exercise with your partner, family member, or friend? How did your discussions help you each better understand where the other one was coming from?

Focus ~ Don't Fuss

Our human culture has developed a remarkable inclination to spend endless time on the figurative and literal gnashing of teeth (TMJ anyone?), obsessing on all the to-do items we think we need to address (headaches, back strains, stiff necks and other joints?), and generally regurgitating topics on a daily basis with no resolution in sight (high blood pressure, ulcers, acid reflux, stomach upsets?). Maintaining this present status quo with regards to our financial position only ensures the draining of tremendous amounts of personal and collective energy and adds great strains on our physical health as well. So it's time to break these old habits and replace them now with a deceptively simple, yet very effective, approach:

1. Set aside certain times of the week to address financial matters and then devote 100% attention of your attention in those moments. You may not reach a conclusion or choice at any one given time, however you will experience (and thereby learn) that *there is no need to carry the subject matter with you all the time and interfere with being peacefully present in other activities.*

2. Select the goal, purchase, planning step, etc. that you need to consider, do your research and identify choices (with the assistance of applicable professionals as necessary), and *take thoughtful, conscious action based on your overall intentions and purposes.*

3. Celebrate the accomplishment of that particular step or phase, and participate in gratitude for the guidance and results of your efforts.

4. Move on fully to your next area of consideration. If you've carefully done your research and reviewed choices in light of your priorities and intentions, then you no longer need to use up extra energy second guessing yourself or wondering if you could have gotten a 'better deal' based on what someone else later claims they did or achieved for a purchase or transaction.

Discovering how best to build your own spiritual guide relationships and then trusting yourself and that interaction is a major part of maintaining, growing and managing your personal energy and effectiveness. *When you find yourself too mired in rehashing (or procrastinating) with financial details, take the step up to the 10,000 feet level to review the perspective on your life and revisit the four steps above to support your focus.* The perpetual fussing will be eliminated from your financial and other life decisions, and you will have a great deal more energy and enthusiasm for accomplishing the truly important purposes in your life. <u>Say 'yes' to more internal peace and balance!</u>

Section Questions:

What is a major blocking point for me in focusing on financial decisions: not doing solid research, forgetting to set priorities first, avoiding making a choice among options, listening too much to outside opinions, not setting aside special time to focus, fear of making the 'wrong' decision, or other issue?

What can and will I do with the extra time and energy I regain from not fussing any more with financial matters?

How can I guide my own input into conversations with partner/family/ friends to support the 'Focus - Don't Fuss' approach in our daily lives?

Create Original Outcomes

When it comes to making a financial decision, whether for a specific event or for a long term plan, the concept of thinking outside the box for the solution that best meets your needs is very applicable and extremely important. Many times I hear people say that 'Oh, that's the industry norm' or "That's what's common" in a situation, as if what's normal or usual or common means that there are no other options available or there's no support for pursuing a preferred alternative.

For example, an acquaintance was interested in opening their first restaurant offering and had been looking for a long time for an appropriate location to rent. They finally found a good spot, although larger than planned, and signed a three-year lease on the property without outside advisement or negotiation. When asked about such a long term, expensive commitment (to property they didn't own and for a first time restaurant venture that was far from a guaranteed success), they answered that 'it was common in the industry to have to take such a long lease and they couldn't afford to lose out on yet another chance.'

I sincerely hoped for their long term success, however they placed a tremendous financial burden on themselves for an extended period of time with no exit strategy in place for a brand new venture. Their feelings of frustration and impatience overrode other options that would have provided them with more flexibility and much less financial exposure. Even negotiating down to a two-year lease or cancellation clause of some type would have saved them tens of thousands of dollars and much anxiety during an already stressful start-up period. Having to meet this large fixed financial commitment influenced the style and operations of this restaurant, and put pressure on them to make some subsequent choices that really didn't match with their original vision and comfort zones.

In another example, a couple decided their top priority was to move to another town to benefit from a specific school district for their children's education. When they received an offer on their house after a few months, they were unhappy with the terms the buyers had submitted and decided not to even respond with a counteroffer because they weren't going to 'give their home away' and they were also feeling too pressed with other events to get into any back and forth discussion. They assumed that it was common for buyers to be deliberately unreasonable in their offers and weren't aware it was possible to negotiate an entire package of terms (price, dates, deposits, etc.)

They received no further offers during the ensuing four months of being on the market. However, this couple could actually have tapped into a couple of other options that may well have resulted in their original desired outcome of getting themselves and the kids into a new home before the new school year started, including:

1. They could have decided to make at least one counteroffer and then not proceed further if the process truly seemed unproductive at that point.

2. They could have countered the proposed sale price with a figure not quite as high as they originally wanted, but included a closing date that better accommodated their own moving needs.

3. They could have reviewed their listing price once again with their agent to make sure the home wasn't actually overpriced for the current market conditions (turns out it was) but, if not, verified comparable prices with documentation to show the buyers.

4. They could have talked about how much value it would be to them to have a cash deal to work with (as these buyers proposed) and reduced the listing price in their own minds accordingly to offset the potential problems with another future buyer who may well have needed to go through a mortgage and appraisal process for a loan.

When entering any new and/or pivotal financial situation, take a bit of time to step back from a decision making deadline to give yourself space, and permission, to brainstorm about options and alternative approaches. That's also a key time to consider tapping into the professional expertise available through financial planners and coaches so they can share both their own personal experiences plus solutions that have worked for many other people in differing circumstances. *Stepping into the realm of considering different paths and tools to accomplish your true, core goals and priorities will provide you with the opportunity to design, create, and choose from a larger set of options – and the resulting outcome will be much more aligned with the intentions that are vital to your own personal needs and purposes.*

So, the next time you feel tempted or pressured to make a choice that's not really in sync with your gut instinct or best interests, try inserting phrases into the discussion such as "How about adjusting that to…" or "Could we modify that…" or "How can we do this too…" or "Let's substitute for this…" ~ and see for yourself what a meaningful difference this approach can make!

Section Questions:

What feelings or thoughts in past financial decisions might have prevented you from checking into other terms or options that could have been to your benefit (uncertainty, lack of knowledge, impatience, fear of missing out, etc.)?

What new reminder(s) can you create for yourself to allow time for asking more questions, getting information, or taking more time for a final decision (two day waiting period, run ideas past a trusted expert, re-visit your priorities list, etc.)?

How can you encourage your partner/family/kids to join you in giving more consideration to options and alternatives in regular discussions?

Research, Decide, Move on

Financial products and tools change constantly these days, with different marketing terms, advertising strategies, and features touted regularly. While sometimes there are truly helpful, legitimate improvements and benefits for the consumer, often the main intention is simply to get people's attention with the latest 'best' deal, new 'instant solution', or 'once in a lifetime' opportunity. These particular approaches are used to generate sales and economic benefits for the provider company and reinforce an environment of snap decisions, fear of missing out, pressures to get ahead in comparison to others, and continual anxiety about making 'right' choices.

As people listen to the daily barrages of such pitches, it's very common to experience analysis paralysis, buyers' remorse, second guessing, investing resources in products that don't really fulfill your needs, or constantly swapping out financial tools with hopes of gaining ground while actually barely maintaining status quo or actually slipping backwards. *Participating in this externally-generated atmosphere really messes with your personal vibrations, energy reservoir, and short circuits your ability to create a life focused on your precious purposes.*

I encourage you to make time for some solid personal financial education, locating objective service professionals, building personal relationships with those individuals and the firms that provide the actual products and tools, and making thoughtful choices that allow you to select the appropriate option for your own situation and then move forward with confidence.

For example, you've decided that it's time to purchase a home so you can expand your business space and foster those pets you've always wanted to. Your personal research takes place over a couple of months and you decide on two particular neighborhoods for your area of focus that comfortably fall within your overall budget considerations. Over the years you have built a good reputation with the local credit union with your personal and business banking needs, and in turn the bank has proven to have really good customer service and also specializes in making (and servicing) home loans in the region. And, after talking with a couple of area realtors about their companies and experience in the neighborhoods, you select one to serve as your buyer agent who best seems to match your communication style and has a reputation for following-through on her work. Since you have an established relationship with your credit union, it's quick and easy to get a pre-approval letter to use when submitting a purchase offer and you know you qualify for a competitive interest rate.

It takes a bit of searching and negotiating but you end up with a great house in your desired location, within your planned budget, and the closing process is well-coordinated with the local providers. Your planning work has paid off in the result you wanted with a pleasant, synchronized experience. If you ever have a question or problem with your mortgage payment, the local administration contact is easily available – plus the addition of your mortgage to your overall banking profile entitles you to preferred benefits with the credit union.

A little while after you close on the house, a work colleague tells you that he 'saved a ton of money' in his own house hunt by playing off a couple of realtors against each other for commission cuts and going with an online financial institution just so he could get an interest rate that was .30 of a point less than the local banks. He ended up buying a larger, more expensive home than they originally thought, but he says it's quite impressive, is sure to be a good investment, and the savings from his realtor/lender strategies were necessary to make the deal work. When you ask about their previous plans for children, your colleague shrugs and replies that he and his partner will wait longer to think about having children so they can both keep working at their current jobs and cover the increased house expenses.

You, however, feel no need to revisit your own transaction for a 'do over' and you have no plans to hop on the refinance bandwagon right away to follow small interest rate shifts. It comes as no surprise to you that you later overhear a conversation around town where your colleague is referred to as a 'pain in the butt' client for his extensive haggling and attitude…nor that your colleague is steaming about errors on his mortgage statement that are taking up considerable time to reach a human representative for resolution. You give yourself a pat on the back for planning well for your *own personal situation* and keeping your focus during your own buying process. You can now simply enjoy your new home, growing business, and furry companions.

When you take the opportunity to look at your financial matters in a comprehensive and holistic way, you will be freed from making individual financial decisions in a haphazard way or in an isolated vacuum. Your choices can be well coordinated with your priorities, intentions, and goals. You will clearly see how all steps will work together to support your plan and your monetary resources will be used effectively and efficiently to provide the desired results. And there will be harmony for, and between, all individuals involved in and affected by your particular financial needs.

This is indeed a far preferable outcome for your own personal life. However, you are also providing a vital message to the financial and media industries, and cultural environment in general, that there is a powerful demand for healthier, better aligned approaches that will support suppliers dedicated to this focus. Just as we have seen the influence of the demand for healthier, more accessible food builds support for the supply of local/organic/natural/fresh offerings from companies large and small, so too can financial-related services be equally impacted in the coming years. Each effort to make financial decisions with greater awareness and conscious choice has a significant ripple effect on the positive energies of all people, and we all appreciate and benefit from your commitment in this area — whether seen or unseen presently by human eyes.

As you do your conscious financial planning and periodic reviews, the steps of research, decide and move on will serve you well by preserving your energies, keeping your vibrational focuses high, and allowing you to invest even more into the other vital areas of your life. In fact, knowing that you have accomplished a better job in handling your financial matters will increase your self-affirmation and propel you to additional meaningful experiences in all areas of your life. Acknowledge your learning experiences and apply the lessons gratefully in your new endeavors.

Section Questions:

What financial situations in the past have caused you to second-guess your decision or express regret over that chosen option?

In hindsight, why were you no longer comfortable with those choices?

What different outlook or action might have helped you make another choice (advance planning, assessing your priorities, more information/ education, better communications, or other)?

How can you use these insights to refine your future personal decision-making process to better match your new life focuses?

Role Model Service

It is impossible to pour from an empty cup, so it's imperative that you take the time to develop your internal guidance system and boundaries before stepping into the role of serving others – as individuals, community involvement, or specific charitable work. You can only be genuinely effective in external service if your own personal house is in order and is securely built on a solid foundation. Keep in mind that a role model is someone defined as "an example, a hero, a mentor, a teacher in the highest regard."

I have met with so many clients over the years who come in distraught but still fully determined to help out relatives or pick up the financial pieces for adult children while their own financial lives are in shambles…little or no savings, increasing debt, unsatisfactory employment situations, deferred personal dreams, unhealthy living arrangements, significant health issues, and more. And there are others who are convinced they need to financially provide everything for their younger children that they themselves never had, so the kids won't have to work so hard or do without what everyone else has or turn out not loving the parents because they were 'deprived.' Still others are well intentioned individuals who donate extensive time and money to charitable endeavors under the unvoiced impression that they need to impoverish themselves to be considered truly worthy and caring members of society.

The only energy source that we have any real personal control over is ourselves. When our personal energy is strong, aligned, and focused, we naturally contribute so very, very much – an incredibly beneficial situation for both ourselves and the world's vibrations and future. It is not selfish to come from a place of authentic integrity, strength, wellness, compassion, and personal power; this is, in fact, a core mission to experience and master during our universal journeys.

Gentle Reminder: As you gain increasing confidence and experience in your own financial realm, you will likely feel excited to share what you've learned and how wonderful the new rewards really can be. Please remember, though, that while you can be a supporting resource for others, now is not the time to unthinkingly fall into trying to convert or convince friends, family, colleagues, or neighbors that what you have personally discovered is also the 'new truth' for them as well. You have a great capacity to share information and experiences with them, and focusing on being a role model for creating personal paths will be most effective and appropriate for all concerned.

Section Questions:

What do I need to change in my own life first to better serve others later?

What new energies and vibrations will I create when I put greater focus on my own experiences and learning?

How will being a stronger role model better help and educate those close to me?

Financial Abundance Opening Meditation

- I come to this moment open to new insights, guidance, and ideas

- That will help me personally move into my own unique purposes.

- I agree to acknowledge and experience any challenging thoughts, feelings and emotions that arise now,

- Letting them flow on past - And to understand that I am not the sum of my past fears or experiences.

- I commit to remain open to the universal love and intuition available here,

- And to absorb increasing quantities of that love and trust into myself day by day.

- I come prepared today to actively learn and take my own steps in co-creating the abundance intended for me;

- And I trust that the information and resources I need will be provided through this state of awareness.

- I give thanks for all the many blessings already in my life,

- And am especially grateful for the spirits here now to assist me in my discoveries.

- So Be It.

Manage Emotional Drivers

If there's one area that will most quickly derail the best intentions and plans in the world, it's the reactive nature of our emotional drivers. For example, as I began writing this section I had a strong urge for a mid-morning snack. I started thinking about what would taste good and then suddenly it dawned on me that I had just finished such a snack only about 15 minutes before. When I paused for a moment, I realized that I didn't actually need to physically eat more and I didn't want to get into an unhealthy pattern of mindlessly slurping down food while writing – so what was it that was really triggering this urge for another snack? This pause made me aware that it was a grey, rainy, cold day and I was also antsy from sitting still from a few hours of writing already. So, I saved my file and got up to make a favorite cup of tea instead. I also decided to do some physical movement and stretching too to release some good endorphins and support my body's need for action. Do I always make such an inspired 'save' around food? Certainly not. But my figurative batting average gets better and better over time as I continue to be mindful of how easy it can be to react to passing thoughts, feelings and emotions.

We've all experienced reactive financial choices, whether through impulsive buying to secure affection, impatience leading to the easiest option, denying another person a purchase or compromise because of annoyance or anger, or acquiring possessions to fill an emotional void. You know…the moment when you feel your self-control just snap and words fly out of your mouth, when you say 'what the heck' and grab for any answer, or literally throw your hands up in frustration and walk away from a situation. Oftentimes we reach this moment when we know we're already bone tired, stressed out, feel put upon, or under pressure to make yet one more choice. Clearly, these types of responses to key relationship, financial, or health issues lead only to further complications and outcomes for the future.

While you can't put off critical decisions indefinitely, taking a short 'time out' to get in touch with your true emotional triggers and re-think your intentions is a straightforward step to increase your success of aligning conscious choices with your true priorities. When you commit yourself to more honest awareness and introspection, it really does become a healthier, more thoughtful habit that can create greater options and beneficial decisions pretty quickly.

Learning to push your own personal 'pause' button regarding financial decisions can take form in many ways; it just depends on what raises your awareness and attention levels and what works well in your particular lifestyle. Some options include:

- Set up a certain waiting period for making purchases depending on your income resources (i.e., one day for items up to $50, a week for items up to $500, etc.)

- When you are shopping online and feeling pressure to make a choice, put items in your virtual cart and then walk away from your computer for an hour or two before pushing the buy button

- Revisit your current spending/savings plan first to ensure you actually have the funds available for the new product or service you are considering

- When you know you are feeling upset, then promise yourself it's window shopping only that day – and that you can return for an actual purchase at a later date

- Have an advance discussion with your partner or family before setting out to a store or showroom for a big ticket item so emotional factors don't overtake the entire situation

- When family or friends approach you for a purchase, loan, or other monetary outlay, let them know you always take 'x' amount of time to consider such requests and you will let them know at a future date

- Ask for more information about a product or service if you are unsure of the real benefits and whether it's really applicable to your priorities – and get yourself comfortable to assert your right to NOT make a decision on the spot

- Before participating in a meeting about finances (family discussion, legal proceedings, investment choices, and the like) understand whether a decision is truly a time-sensitive matter during that specific time or it's more simply driven by another party's preference to get something wrapped up

- Keep your key priorities for a specific outcome at the top of your mind to avoid the trap of caving in to another choice because you suddenly felt overwhelmed or confused with additional information coming at you

- When you become aware that much of your concern surrounds a bunch of what if's or general anxiety, re-affirm that you have plenty of spiritual support and guidance available – and 'don't go borrowing trouble' which likely will never cross your doorstep

In summary, assess the true emotional state or reason for your financial decision as honestly as possible and understand that you can let any undesired feelings flow through and release <u>before </u>making a final decision. *Adding this step actually decreases the overall time involved in making a thoughtful, conscious choice, as you eliminate complications and conflicting options early on and can more easily move-on to your next focus without regrets, bad feelings, or second guessing your decision.*

Section Questions:

What are my own particular emotional 'hot buttons' that tend to impact my key choices around relationships, health, and finances?

What new tools can I begin to use now that will help me minimize the times I make a decision based heavily on these emotional drivers?

How will this different awareness free up more time and energy for the really important focuses in my life?

Affirming Communication with Partners, Family, and Children

<u>Perception is reality for each of us</u> – so honor your own current perspective and feelings while stretching your comfort zone with information, professional resources, and new habits. Extend the same courtesy to your partners, family members and friends as they are in a place of learning and adjusting too. As any good communications coach will share with you, avoid using phrases during conversations that imply responses are 'illogical, immature, off-base, unreasonable, makes no sense, and the like." If the true basis of a concern or fear is not discussed, then there can be no resulting healing or adoption of new outlooks – individually or between people.

Even more important than the specific words you use is the energy/state of mind that you actually bring to the table during conversations. If you choose certain words to sound as though you are trying to be 'reasonable' but your energy and physical position are really in a different place (i.e. condescending, anxious, angry, fearful, manipulative, untrusting, etc.) then there will be a great disconnect in positive vibrational states and little of benefit accomplished. *Energy does not lie – and so must be the prevailing consideration in any genuine connection you seek.* It would be far more productive to put more emphasis on all parties understanding that a safe, neutral zone is intended for every one and that immediate resolution to questions does not have to occur at the moment of conversation.

When we're not accustomed to talking about financial matters, you may initially feel tired or somewhat anxious as everyone experiences tension, differences of opinion, and varying personal preferences. It may seem easier to try an 'indirect' approach, such as opaquely implying what you mean but hoping others guess your real intention...or saying you'll defer to another person but actually retaining your own fear or anger or resentment...or pulling up those old limiting labels (discussed earlier under Ditch the Limiting Labels) such as "I'm really dumb about financial matters, but...." However there really is no effective substitute for being as honest and open as possible. It is far preferable to stumble around a bit with your wording and trust that your truly sincere intention will provide the good energy for your part of the conversation.

If you and/or your partner or family members aren't comfortable or ready to meet yet in such a discussion, then enlisting the assistance of a qualified coach or counselor initially may help you all learn and practice healthy, uplifting approaches. These may include making time to talk about individual and mutual priorities, alternating initiating conversations or making financial choices, and regularly setting aside dedicated 'safe' space to hold conversations. Scheduling specific times to hold conversations allows 'soak time' in between discussions so each person can absorb what was talked about, and also promotes some advance preparation (via thinking or note writing) about topics that each participant would like to address. The need to think about financial choices throughout each day is also minimized as you'll know that dedicated time is available to more fully and effectively consider the issues at hand for the week.

To help set the stage for your discussions, here are some other tips you can use:

- Organize your paperwork in one location, using folders/ binders/fire box/cloud for storage options

- Keep an updated list of professional advisers and their contact information

- Include items such as passwords, legal documents. health care instructions, a list of regular expenses and payment back-up, most recent account statements, and similar papers that you may need to access quickly. Don't rely solely on your respective memory capabilities, which may freeze up during stressful situations.

- Update this summary file annually or after major changes so current information is easily available

- Schedule financial meetings with planners, investment managers, accountants, and others so that both/all partners can attend. Each person's input and understanding in these meetings is equally important.

- Hold an annual 'State of the Family' address to keep everyone informed of the overall goals and financial picture you're all working with

Section Questions:

What space in our home can I set aside or designate as a 'chill zone' to create more open productive financial conversations? Or is there an outdoor location that would work just as well or even better for us?

What is a special day and time that we can build into our schedule as a focused, regular opportunity to discuss financial decisions, touch base on priorities and goals, and review any actions steps needed?

How will the new synergies and combined energy of all partners help expand the financial abundance and decision-making process in your life – individually and as a whole?

Path of Increasing Finesse

You've embarked on a new path of perspective in creating your own personal financial philosophy and manifestation. Like any other life path, you will find some ups and downs, changes in terrain, unexpected events, and ever-changing views. As you observe your personal vibrations changing (perhaps along the Emotional Guidance Scale offered by Abraham Hicks as a resource), you will increasingly sense manifestation results rather than trying to measure them in pure quantitative ways. Periodic reviews of your priorities and intentions will flow more easily and your awareness of making conscious choices will continue to become more highly tuned as well. You will become open to the greater number of options available to you in situations, yet your decision-making process will be simpler and more rewarding with the new tools and skills you are employing. This is all part of the increasing finesse you are developing minute by minute, day by day – and those seemingly tiny steps add up to magnificent new creations.

Such a committed path to co-creating your abundances may sometimes seem to take longer or be less obvious than what you were familiar with in your previous focus. Maybe you were used to pushing through multiple obstacles to reach a desired goal, but now recognize that universal timing needs to be a balancing component to your action steps. Or you now more often embrace that solutions or gifts coming to you, while perhaps not always exactly what you first specified, are indeed for your highest and best interests – and you will cherish those even more. *Your daily yardstick for fulfillment becomes the enjoyment and experience in each moment rather than being in perpetual motion with an ever-changing to-do list to accomplish.*

Some of these changes will likely generate feelings of discomfort and the questioning of many paradigms. Understand that you are certainly not alone in experiencing new emotional reactions, instances of mental fatigue, and different physical sensations. There will be times when you need to concentrate on periods of rest, healing, processing, and adjusting before launching forward again. These periods of inner reflection are equally important as the periods of decisions and actions steps. Balance and trust are two of the most important factors to develop as you move along your current path and entire life journey.

When I'm starting to feel a bit discouraged or impatient or uncertain about the outcomes of the life purposes I've embraced, there are a few key phrases I bring forth…perhaps these will be of assistance to you too:

- Don't give up five minutes before the miracle occurs

- There is only one degree of difference between hot water (211 degrees) and boiling water (212 degrees)

- There is no way the results of my life can go backward into previously-experienced undesired outcomes when I've transformed my personal vibrations so dramatically

- Dozens of universal spirits are supporting my authentic life purposes each day for my own personal benefit, for those other lives I touch, and for the world as a whole

- I may be on an uncharted path, but I have the intuition, inner energy, and universal connections to create a joyous experience along the way

Section Questions:

What key phrases can I use in my own life that will help me move forward when I feel stuck or confused?

What daily rituals will I put into place to support my new path and focus?

When I review my successes over the past week, month, and year, what lessons and rewards have I experienced?

Financial Abundance Opening Meditation

- I come to this moment open to new insights, guidance, and ideas

- That will help me personally move into my own unique purposes.

- I agree to acknowledge and experience any challenging thoughts, feelings and emotions that arise now,

- Letting them flow on past - And to understand that I am not the sum of my past fears or experiences.

- I commit to remain open to the universal love and intuition available here,

- And to absorb increasing quantities of that love and trust into myself day by day.

- I come prepared today to actively learn and take my own steps in co-creating the abundance intended for me;

- And I trust that the information and resources I need will be provided through this state of awareness.

- I give thanks for all the many blessings already in my life,

- And am especially grateful for the spirits here now to assist me in my discoveries.

- So Be It.

Thoughtful Planning Mindset

"Money doesn't buy happiness (or anything else of soul import)
but it does provide options for us here on this planet – so there
are many reasons to earn and use the tool of money wisely."
-Financial Stewardship (2014)

Even as we have faith in a universal presence, available guidance, and protections, we know it is not incompatible to use our own appropriate safety and planning measures when driving a car, boating, crossing a street, consuming food and drink, etc. Likewise, finances are an integral part of our lives and merit the same consideration and application of appropriate tools when available. *Financial stewardship is about engaging in financial education and planning in the spirit of flexibility, priorities and conscious choices…and taking action steps to support our best energies and intentions while here as a human being.* As we use our monetary resources in thoughtful, authentic ways that reflect our highest values, we will be of great service to ourselves, the environment, animals, and other people by living 'in-sync with purpose.'

To help illustrate the message of this section let's look at the familiar story of embarking on a timeless, iconic 'Road Trip'.

You begin with the idea to journey to a distant, desired destination and then proceed to list and review your current resources (money, vehicle, gas, provisions, companions, etc.) You tap into chosen contacts for guidance (AAA, internet research and ratings, maps, books and the like), and plan an overview of the landmarks that will be the main focus of the trip. Along the journey, you take side trips as so inspired, recalibrate directions when the inevitable 'oops' occurs, and use newly found tools and tips from fellow travelers. Your past experiences and tales from other travelers remind you to maintain your body in good health and keep other modes of transport in good working order too during all those miles. Your mindset all along was one of personal interest, excitement, rolling with the situation when necessary, and overall anticipation for learning, seeing new people and places, and absorbing the entire experience. And so you did indeed have the really good time you envisioned.

The road trip for your personal financial stewardship can have the same rewarding experience as the physical travel analogy above. As you adopt and apply more of the principles we've shared here, your daily financial mindset will become more thoughtful, comfortable and open to those areas you previously avoided or dealt with only in a fearful, anxious, or stressful way. Here's the corresponding outline for your personal financial journey:

1. Know where you are currently by understanding your spending and savings plan

2. Choose where you want to go by taking a comprehensive look at your priorities, intentions, and desired rewards

3. Tap into independent educational resources for tools and background information

4. Make your decisions and identify actions steps based on your own authentic purpose and balanced implementation

5. Periodically review your location/status and adjust your personal direction as needed to account for new goals, information, and available resources

And here are some individual points to keep in mind that will help you continue to move into, and expand, your thoughtful planning mindset:

- The financial component of a situation is only one consideration in decision-making…other significant reasons should be present and of high priority as deciding factors

- We rarely can pinpoint time of our passing from human life, however engaging in fear-filled decisions is the antithesis of our purpose (i.e., please view insurance as a future care and flexibility option rather than as a prevention of illness or death)

- Choose savings and certain protection tools as a balance to daily carpe diem consciousness.

- Keep it simple and make life long choices, not going overboard while planning to the detriment of present purpose and awareness

- Support your as yet unknown and unseen opportunities by a thoughtful allocation of resources mindset ~ the direct opposite of the customary saving for rainy day (the other shoe might drop) or for a retirement period when we otherwise believe fewer abundances will be provided

- View the presence of others' monetary resources as gifts available to support charitable giving, environmental preservation, family/ pet survivor care, and more

- Focus on straightforward, proportional implementation of plans to minimize or mitigate life's potentially otherwise harmful outcomes

- Add true economic and personal value through your business propositions (versus paper money and market accounting which produce a false illusion of gain and substance)

- Make financial education a priority to gain empowerment, relief from anxiety, personal openness, increased vibrational levels and energetic freedom

Get Back to the Basics

I've included this section as a high-level outline to show a continuum of tools and steps to begin (or enhance) your own financial stewardship planning. There may be items that need to be addressed simultaneously (hence our emphasis on the importance of a comprehensive review so you're not working at cross-purposes with your efforts) or you may be able to address certain other items on a stand-alone basis. Either way, everyone's personal situation will be different and custom solutions are available to maximize your own benefits and best support your unique purposes. So please do seriously consider enlisting the assistance of a professional financial planner periodically so you can avail yourself of new information and perspectives. Attending local workshops (those planned as interactive, educational events with no investment strings attached) on financial literacy and topics specific to your personal situation are also potentially helpful resources too. And check out the Fundamental Resources section of this book for some tried and true web sites that include current articles, printable PDF files, general consumer suggestions, and many other informative tools.

Thinking back to our actual road trip example (covered in the prior section), if you decided you would be travelling via your personal vehicle and staying at a combination of local lodging and with friends, then you would include phone calls to the friends and selected B&Bs in your planning process. Spending time researching campgrounds, obtaining airline schedules, or figuring out how to pay for five star hotels would not be on your radar at all…getting involved in that data would be just a diversion of your time and brain power.

The same process applies for your financial planning needs. If you don't have some solid foundation tools in place first, it's not a productive use of your energy to get immersed in more sophisticated or risky matters (regardless of any current media hype). You also would not be well served by trying to select, for example, a particular insurance or investment product before you have first thoughtfully determined your goals and what your budgets can be.

Please always keep in mind that large life transitions, such as divorce, widowhood, career change, inheritances, children, new business ventures, or medical conditions will generate very different needs with some immediate considerations to be addressed.

Basics Group 1

- ✓ Checking account and beginning reserve/emergency saving account
- ✓ Credit report review and FICO score (at least annually)
- ✓ Current personal budget
- ✓ File or box with pertinent financial information easily accessible
- ✓ Healthcare proxy (ages 18 and up), Living will, Basic will and guardianship provisions (for minors and companion animals)
- ✓ Annual review of financial position: income, expenses, assets, debts, new goals/options/alternatives, bank statements, etc.
- ✓ Family 'state of the union' updates and regular discussions
- ✓ One credit card ($1,000 +/-) for restricted purposes (i.e., car/plane reservation for family emergency travel or first time credit establishment)
- ✓ Minimum insurance for vehicles and renters' possessions

- ✓ Basic term life insurance to provide for immediate needs for partner, children, companion animals, repayment of loans, etc.
- ✓ Health insurance through work, state exchange, federal programs, or local chamber/membership group

Basics Group 2

- ✓ Expanded reserve savings account
- ✓ Specific purpose savings accounts (travel, car purchase/repair, etc.)
- ✓ Increased amounts of term insurance coverage
- ✓ Upgraded auto insurance coverage
- ✓ Homeownership options explored if desired
- ✓ Homeowners and umbrella insurance policies
- ✓ Retirement plan participation at work
- ✓ Disability, dental, vision insurances through work
- ✓ Review income tax information for significant work and family events

Intermediate Group 1

- ✓ Retirement account for self-employed business owners
- ✓ Self-employed disability policy
- ✓ Beginning education savings for self and/or children
- ✓ Beginning investment account(s) outside of retirement savings (primarily mutual fund emphasis)
- ✓ Long term care insurance policy options for individuals and business owners
- ✓ Budget conscious travel, recreational vehicles, hobbies, etc.
- ✓ Annual tax projection for significant personal changes and pre-year end planning opportunities

Intermediate Group 2

- ✓ Expanding education savings funds
- ✓ Expanded investment account saving and diversification
- ✓ Expanded insurance options such as universal life, whole life, hybrid products
- ✓ Second home/vacation/rental property considered
- ✓ Higher end discretionary travel, boats, hobbies, etc.
- ✓ Estate planning advice from CPA, CFP and attorney (asset protection, charitable giving, income planning, inheritances, etc.)

Advanced/Specialty Group

- ✓ Special needs trusts (support for individuals with extensive medical and/or supervisory needs)
- ✓ Family/marital trusts to manage inheritance and legacy provisions
- ✓ Business succession planning
- ✓ Custom active management investment accounts
- ✓ Specialty investment vehicles and international scope
- ✓ Higher concentration of individual stock(s) in portfolio
- ✓ High-end insurance products and strategies
- ✓ Reverse mortgage product for ages 62+ (both for lower and high income individuals)
- ✓ Ownership of multiple investment properties

Financial Abundance Opening Meditation

- I come to this moment open to new insights, guidance, and ideas

- That will help me personally move into my own unique purposes.

- I agree to acknowledge and experience any challenging thoughts, feelings and emotions that arise now,

- Letting them flow on past - And to understand that I am not the sum of my past fears or experiences.

- I commit to remain open to the universal love and intuition available here,

- And to absorb increasing quantities of that love and trust into myself day by day.

- I come prepared today to actively learn and take my own steps in co-creating the abundance intended for me;

- And I trust that the information and resources I need will be provided through this state of awareness.

- I give thanks for all the many blessings already in my life,

- And am especially grateful for the spirits here now to assist me in my discoveries.

- So Be It.

Concluding Thoughts

As we wrap up here, I'd like to share with you an important caution regarding the "Yeah, but…" syndrome which can affect all of us at any time, sometimes more so than others, regardless of our physical location or condition. Symptoms also appear with phrases such as, "I completely understand/hear what you're say, but you wouldn't believe how they keep treating me…" or "I get what you're saying, but you don't fully understand how unique my own situation is…" or "That might work for other people, but I can't change this because…" and every other possible version of the sentiment. This can be a highly contagious condition but it is possible to inoculate yourself against the most harmful effects by applying very honest personal awareness and intention.

Although we may diligently study and review all of the potential personal blocks provided in this book and our other studies, many a good affirmation or intention has been waylaid, set aside, or otherwise dropped by talking ourselves out of action – whether through unbalanced overthinking, taking comfort in the appointed rules of normal life (reality?), or trying to preserve the fearful part of our individual ego by distancing ourselves from universal principles.

Everyone has the ability through free choice to change their personal story in any and every way they can envision ~ including YOU. *To move beyond the 'Yeah, but' syndrome and into the straight 'Yeah, let's do this' mode, we take all the mind learning and combine it with a healthy dose of heart input. Including your heart perspective will introduce the strengths of passion, trust, love, faith, and balanced persistence.* The infinite circle can again be complete between mind, body, and soul for each and every choice you make.

Possible antidotes to help you move away from this syndrome include statements such as:

- ✓ "Well, that's a new idea and I'm not sure how it can apply to myself at the moment, however I'll keep an open mind and keep listening to spirit nudges and messages."

- ✓ "I don't understand what this message means to me at the moment, however I do know it was given to me for a particular reason so I'll let it 'simmer' for a bit and ask for more clarity during meditations."

- ✓ "I really don't like the message I'm hearing, however I may need to be more honest with myself and thoughtfully remember that the information I get from trusted universal sources really is for my best interest long-term."

- ✓ "I'm feeling overwhelmed/scared/anxious to make this change, however I know I can receive plenty of spiritual support and more peace while I take things step by step."

- ✓ "I feel like just shutting out this idea right now, however since I'm aware of this feeling I choose to respond differently and take some time to consider my options from a more balanced viewpoint."

I greatly appreciate the opportunity to share all this bridge information with you and thank you for taking the initiative to embrace financial stewardship further into your life. I deeply believe that the Law of Attraction abundances are ready, waiting, and available for each of us right now. And that it is indeed very possible to co-create lives for ourselves in the 'now-here' where we experience the peace, joy and depth of understanding in our personal purposes and our universal connections.

Transformation happens from the inside outward. Each of us is our own unique power cord to universal energy and community. By maintaining a high quality connection and remaining fully plugged-in, the incredible transforming energy is delivered to us abundantly. So, quite literally then, from my heart to yours, May the Force be with You ~ and in You!

Laurie, November 2015

Fundamental Resources

Certified Financial Planner Board, www.cfp.net, www.LetsMakeAPlan.org

Financial Planning Association, www.fpanet.net

National Association of Personal Financial Advisors, www.napfa.org

My Money (Financial Literacy & Education Commission), www.mymoney.gov

Consumer Financial Protection Board, www.consumerfinance.gov

Directions for Women, www.DirectionsForWomen.com

Math for Grownups, www.MathForGrownups.com

EverPlans Life Resources, www.EverPlans.com

Five Wishes Living Will and discussion booklet, www.AgingWithDignity.org

Financial Literacy, American Institute of CPAs, www.360FinancialLiteracy.org www.feedthepig.org

Understanding Taxes, American Institute of CPAs, www.360Taxes.org

Long Term Care (US Dept. of Health and Human Services), www.LongTermCare.gov

Financial Aid (US Dept. of Education), www.Ed.gov

Elder Care Resources & Locator (US Administration on Aging), www.ElderCare.gov

Financial Professional Designations (FINRA) Different credentials required for different services and product offerings) www.finra.org/investors

Annual Credit Report (Tip: alternate between the three reporting agencies throughout the year so you can actually check every few months at no cost), www.annualcreditreport.com

Financial Decisions Review List

- ❖ Own Your Financial Story
- ❖ Change Your Financial Story
- ❖ Ditch the Limiting Labels
- ❖ Count Your Blessings
- ❖ Understand Your Needs
- ❖ Understand the Cost of Options
- ❖ Keep It Simple Sweetie
- ❖ Mutual Fair Value
- ❖ Priorities and Intentions
- ❖ Focus, Don't Fuss
- ❖ Create Personal Outcomes
- ❖ Research, Decide, Move On
- ❖ Role Model Service
- ❖ Emotional Drivers
- ❖ Affirming Communications
- ❖ Path of Increasing Finesse
- ❖ Thoughtful Planning Mindset

BONUS

Meditation Assistance

44 Word and Message Deck

(Re-published from Financial Stewardship: A Guide to Personal
Financial Health and Wellness [©2014])

These forty-four words and messages are included here as an integral part
for specific guidance and examples of how to establish your own personal
financial stewardship and understand what it really means to you.

Each word and message combination has been placed on separate page,
so you can easily invoke the spirit of card reading by either envisioning a
number from 1 to 44 at the time you wish to read, or state your intention
and open to a page as you feel led.

You can also simply read through the following pages for additional
considerations and insights: one per day, one per week, or straight through
as you prefer.

ONE: Accountability

Personal accountability is the key to an honest and true relationship with yourself and your impact on others in your care. Learning about your finances and educating yourself on appropriate choices are within everyone's ability and responsibility, so find unbiased sources of information for the decisions you need to make. Think about the longer term effects of those choices…not simply about the short term benefits. Not considering both timeframes may lead you to ignore or overlook options that would really be the best solution for your own personal situation. Your finances are unique to your own situation and should not be automatically compared to what others are doing.

Consider:

How can I address the fears I may have about financial issues?

How do my financial choices tie into my life intentions and ability to achieve those?

How do my decisions impact others around me?

TWO: Balance

Just as with your physical health, a strong core is needed to keep your finances in balance with your overall goals and plans. And also like body core exercises, it's necessary to create regular opportunities to reinforce the financial choices that you believe will keep you in shape for the long term. Each person's needs are different so it is necessary to experiment with different tools to create and customize a plan that will work for you. There is no one best solution for everyone – persevere until you find approaches that resonate with your intentions.

Consider:

What are my goals that require balancing and what are their priorities for me?

How can I creatively and actively achieve them with open thinking?

Have any of my goals changed and I now need to re-balance my focus?

THREE: Career

One of the trickiest questions for us is how to choose or integrate our personal passions with the need to earn a living in the physical world. Sometimes it seems that money and following your heart are opposing factors but fully addressing this situation can actually be one of the most enlightening and empowering conversations you can have with yourself. Money is one of many tools here, yet is quite often labeled as good or bad depending on a person's past experiences and perspectives. However, if you are on a path to take you beyond the past and toward new possibilities, you can think outside the box to figure out how to meet both your practical daily needs with your long term callings.

Consider:

Can I be an effective contributor to the universal needs within a traditional career position?

If I feel the need to choose or develop an alternate path, how can I do so with a responsible focus on also meeting healthy physical world needs?

Are there different phases in my life when I adjust my focus and involvement to reflect changes in my learning and journey?

FOUR: Choices

Making conscious choices in our lives is the basis of honoring our intentions and callings. And the area of financial stewardship is an integral part of that process. It's just as important to consider these decisions and choices as it is to review your physical health or relationships because finances influence many of our thoughts and communications, whether consciously or otherwise. Having a healthy dialogue about money choices can reflect positively on our personal relationships, our work alternatives, meeting future goals, our personal power and impact, how we can help change future community conversations about financial issues, and much more.

Consider:

How do I give choices about financial matters a lower priority in my life - and why and when?

What other areas of my life are affected by my choices (or lack thereof) regarding money?

What benefits could I have by taking a more active role in the financial stewardship of my life?

FIVE: Commitment

Making a commitment to a person or action becomes part of our personal contract and journey. Choosing those commitments is then an important reflection on who we are and where our focus will be going forward. When we make the commitment to be financial stewards for our own lives we acknowledge both the gifts and responsibilities that we've been entrusted with. Having the discipline to regularly review our resources and opportunities for using them is an important component of our journey – whether those resources are our time, skills, thoughts, or money. And when we view money as a tool for accomplishing our goals then we can harness that resource from a place of knowledge and strength.

Consider:

How can I renew my commitment to being a steward with my financial resources?

Are there different or new ways I can use these resources to meet my goals?

What can I change in my approach to view my financial commitments in a more effective, positive way?

SIX: Communication

It's often easy to assume that another person will be (or should be) coming from the same view point to understand or agree with a decision we've made. Since we're all coming from our own set of unique experiences, though, it's more likely that some critical pieces of information or perspective may actually not be part of the initial conversation and misunderstanding or conflicts arise at a further time. If people are less accustomed to openly discussing financial issues in a relationship then it's a short path to differing priorities, disagreements about choices, and taking personal judgment positions. Practicing open communication about finances and stewardship – including active listening and thoughtful questions – can be a healthy and loving contribution to both the relationship and each person's life.

Consider:

Do I personally feel comfortable having financial conversations with my family, friends, business partners, and other stakeholders?

How can I continue to gain comfort and knowledge myself and encourage the same for those people important in the process?

What can I change in my communication style that will help everyone in these conversations?

SEVEN: Consistency

When we regularly practice our skills in healing, meditation, journeying, and other services we gain confidence, effectiveness, and spiritual growth. The same benefits are available when we apply a consistent approach to our personal financial planning and management. Whether that consistency is found in ongoing savings, oversight of spending, or adding new knowledge to our tool belt, we continue to transform our decision making and insights into our options. Being consistent with conscious choices gives us a platform from which to launch yet more discoveries and flexibility.

Consider:

What part of my finances could benefit from more consistency and thought?

How can I re-view 'consistency' as a helpful tool in my stewardship?

What is holding me back from making progress toward my financial goals?

EIGHT: Control

There are many tools that can be misused to control situations or people, and money is one such prominent tool. Perceptions of both abundance and scarcity of money can influence relationships, events, health, and the ability to make choices. Behind the need to control is fear and the desire to hold onto a concrete outcome based in past experience. This fear perception can influence us personally in our own actions or be projected on other people to expand a sense of connection in an attempt to validate a desired outcome. By recognizing that money could be an area we use for seeking control, we give ourselves the opportunity to release that fear and open up instead to new paradigms – just as we seek to do by balancing other ego attributes in our lives.

Consider:

Do I have a fear rooted in money that is holding me back from reaching for my goals?

Do I use money directly or in conversations to consciously or unconsciously bind someone else to my perception of an outcome?

Or is someone else trying to use money in some way to supplant my own self-determination and personal path?

NINE: Creativity

There are a few different ways to view the correlation between money and creativity. First, there's the idea that "Money doesn't buy happiness but it does buy options." In this instance, an abundance of this resource that is beyond your needs can give you flexibility and alternatives for investing in things here on earth that will help you meet more of your life goals and those you wish to assist. Second, when you feel there is less actual cash available than you might otherwise prefer, then satisfaction can be found in using what you do have more efficiently and effectively with creative solutions. If you truly do need more resources to meet a healthy life, then in this scenario you also have the opportunity to create new ways to receive additional abundance that is available. Third, when you feel your physical needs are already matched with the resources you have, you have the opportunity to continue your focus on further developing your spiritual growth and creating another new future.

Consider:

Which scenario do you see yourself in now?

Have you been in others during your life and how do you see your transition between them?

How do you specifically determine when you feel are in financial abundance, scarcity, or balance?

TEN: Culture

Our individual perceptions of what money is and what is means has been greatly influenced by our own cultures, religions, histories, and experiences. Verbal or written lessons and exchanges we are given from a young age all mesh together to impact our choices and judgments. Advice that we choose to use may even be contradictory at times, given the broad scope of information we've accumulated over time – and we may not even be consciously aware of what details our mind selects in making an actual decision at a particular time. When you combine these factors for yourself with a partner's or family's input, you end up with ever more infinite possibilities of reactions and responses.

Consider:

What perceptions can I identify from my upbringing and life experiences that might influence my financial decisions?

Do these perceptions still make sense or fit with how I want to envision my future life and choices?

What can I do to be more aware of how I'm making a particular choice with my resources?

ELEVEN: Education

Knowledge is a very powerful tool, and synonyms include awareness, know-how, recognition, enlightenment, discernment, and learning. The stewardship of our finances and resources is an important component of our intentions and contribution during our lifetime. While we cannot be experts in every area, it is always possible to gain some proficiency for important factors in our lives through some application and persistence. Financial stewardship does require commitment and thoughtful consideration, but there is no secret financial kingdom where only a few hold the key to knowledge. Step into your stewardship role through the wide array of educational materials available online, in books, and through objective professionals. Then apply your common sense, understanding of your personal needs and goals, and ownership of your choices.

<u>Consider:</u>

What can I do right now to expand my financial knowledge and strength?

Do I carry excuses or fears that currently prevent me from fully applying the information I already have?

How can I help other family members learn about money choices so they will have this power too?

TWELVE: Enlightenment

As we know from other parts of our lives, enlightenment may arrive in a burst of recognition or in small pieces over time. And the process is a never ending, far reaching one with only our own parameters to limit the experience. Gaining awareness of financial matters and how we make those related decisions is an integral part of our learning to effectively and thoughtfully live on earth. Offering a sincere intention to take further responsibility for our education and choices in this area is the first step to becoming more open and aware of the guidance and resources that are available to us. When you choose to embrace your questions and concerns about financial stewardship you will be provided with the tools and insights you need…reach out and accept what is offered to you and continue to growth in gratitude and strength.

Consider:

Do I give financial stewardship equal balance in the enlightenment I seek?

If not, why do I delay or ignore this particular resource?

How will my life gain balance and purpose when I do spend thoughtful time with this topic?

THIRTEEN: Esteem

When we feel uncertain, vulnerable, or confused about our personal value and purpose it is tempting to reach for external sources to try to validate our egos. This may take various forms, from pursuing more professional titles to building a group of supporters to justifying (or denying) the accumulation of money to fit into a comfortable projection of who we think we should be. It takes a strong and honest conversation with ourselves, not just once but periodically, to review our intentions and question whether we are using money in as a healthy resource or as a crutch for an unresolved need or fear. If we are making decisions – consciously or unconsciously - based on money having a label of good or bad for whatever reasons, then we are limiting and hampering the ability to make more clear and thoughtful decisions about our relationships, work, activities, and future as well.

Consider:

How can I quietly listen to my inner thoughts and feelings to better discern what is influencing my current financial decisions?

Do I take too much comfort in relying on the ways I've made these choices in the past or am I willing to use a different viewpoint?

Is it healthy for me and in sync with my purpose to continue using the perspectives I've had before?

FOURTEEN: Exchange

Money is a tool for us to use to accomplish the goals we have in life. Like our health and natural resources, this requires an approach of gratitude and balance for the gifts we are given to be able to use them wisely and with purpose. Whether we are receiving actual hard currency or are bartering for a good or service, we are exchanging our time, energy, and skill set for another resource to help us achieve what we desire. These are important and valuable parts of ourselves that we are bringing to the table. So it's equally important that we make sure this exchange is valued properly and that we choose to expend our remuneration in ways that bring us healthy support in the context of our long term intention.

Consider:

Am I thoughtfully valuing both my contribution to exchanges and how I allocate what I receive in return?

Do I recognize and understand the true value of what other people offer with their products and services?

Are there inconsistencies or imbalances with how we assign such value in our culture or economy that affects my own personal choices?

FIFTEEN: Fear

Some cultures and families have a history of openly discussing money and making financial conversations a common occurrence. When this history does not exist or conversations have not been balanced, the topic is pressed deeper and deeper into the background and becomes one of those dark areas that inspire discomfort, confusion, and plain fear in our lives. Becoming comfortable and strong with financial stewardship requires that we apply the same approach to finances that we do with other areas we very much wanted to adjust but feared. Finding the tools that work for you from the wide range available is a key part of the exploration, as is learning how to have your own internal conversations in a way that is initially safe and manageable.

Consider:

How can I use the same approach that has already helped me with my health, family, and other concerns to become a better financial steward?

What is my ideal comfort level that I want to envision for making choices with my finances?

What past feelings and experiences have kept me from taking ownership in this area until now?

SIXTEEN: Flexibility

Many financial products and services are often offered as 'the best' or 'the right choice' or some other definitive answer. However, the reality we truly face is that there is little predictability or certainty in the paths our lives take when influenced long term by other people, a global economy, the natural environment, health and medical considerations, and much more. Just as with our perspectives in other areas of our lives, it is ultimately not productive to be locked into one set of expectations or responses from a financial standpoint either. Making considered choices by looking at a range of alternatives and including the factor of flexibility into the process will provide more options for the unknown and unseen factors that will arise throughout your lifetime.

Consider:

What solutions can I choose for my finances that will give me flexibility in 10 years, 20 years, and more?

Do I apply sufficient time and patience when reviewing financial options to make a more informed and thoughtful choice?

How can I find the objective, informative resources I need to understand what's best for my own stewardship efforts?

SEVENTEEN: Gifting

Our hearts lead us to make gifts to family members, service organizations, and other causes which we believe are worthy to support. Part of being a good financial steward is to balance the messages from our hearts with a thoughtful consideration of how those gifts will actually be used and whether a particular gift will support a true need or is really a short term crutch for a want or posturing instead. It is particularly difficult to have this caring but objective view with those people and groups we are emotionally close to, however this is a situation where consideration may be the most important: the fine line between assistance and enabling, our long term financial health and a loved one's current position, an organization's effectiveness and our own direct service.

Consider:

Do I over-gift for my own circumstances in an effort to prove my caring or worth to others?

Would I have a more meaningful impact if I contributed more of my own time and energy rather than a monetary gift?

When I use my money resources for a gift do I have the knowledge and confidence that it will be used well by the recipient too?

EIGHTEEN: Healing

When we've made past decisions about our financial matters that have led to poor or harmful results, it's tempting to just figuratively throw up our hands and either say to ourselves "I just can't handle these kinds of choices so I'll ignore them" or "I've messed up so often before that I'm sure I'll never understand or make better decisions in the future, so why bother." But if you want to be true and consistent with our other stated intentions of continually learning to live a healthier and more rewarding life, then revisiting your experiences with money is an integral part of this process. Denying, hiding, or abdicating responsibility for financial stewardship doesn't generate any better results than those responses do in other areas of our lives. And since finances often affect those other areas, you cannot be fully healed and move forward in truth and joy unless you take time for our stewardship review.

Consider:

What areas of my life are still incomplete without understanding my current financial perspectives?

Do I need to talk with family members or friends about how these perspectives are influencing our lives and choices?

How will healing in the area of financial stewardship help me to move forward with my other goals?

NINETEEN: Health

Your mind, body, and soul all intertwine with the energy you generate and use, so the type and intensity of that energy at its source is critical to all that we are. Healthy financial stewardship is an integral part of making balanced and productive choices in your relationships, career, hobbies, lifestyle, volunteer work, and long term physical health. Becoming more aware of your current thoughts and emotions about finances will help you identify the ones that are reinforcing and spreading negative uses of energy throughout your body and life decisions. When you modify or remove harmful misconceptions, responses, and projections in this area, you will not only make financial decisions that are better for your own personal situation but you will also greatly impact many other areas of your life as well. It's also very important to recognize and reinforce the positive thoughts and energy that you've chosen to adopt in your stewardship, as this is a powerful tool to envision and support your future.

Consider:

How would improving my financial health help with my physical health?

What new steps can I take toward better financial fitness as a responsible steward?

What benefits will I experience in other parts of my life when I put some focus on financial wellness?

TWENTY: Hoarding

Insecurity, fear, and overreliance on past experiences can lead to hoarding of many different resources: tangible property, money, emotions, animals, or human relationships. Trying to compensate for these inner challenges by substituting accumulation or attempted control doesn't solve the true situation – any more than overdoing openness and perpetual giving does on the other end of the spectrum. If you find yourself stuck and unhappy with how your days or relationships pass, then perhaps you are neglecting to use the abundance of resources that are available to provide you with the long term fulfillment you seek.

Consider:

How can I responsibly and productively use my financial and emotional resources to help me reach the goals I seek?

What fears and past wounds are holding me back from moving ahead at this time?

What can I do today in manageable steps to help release myself from feeling the need to over protect the resources I have?

TWENTY-ONE: Honesty

Self-exploration and questioning is one of the greatest opportunities, and challenge, that we have on the search for our potential and understanding our role in the grand universe around us. Even when we do our conscious best, there may still be hidden areas that we cannot see or reach either alone or at the present time. So our intention and expressions of honesty must be treated with both compassion and the acceptance of imperfect knowledge to help balance us in our personal and world views. While we need to stay in touch with our inner voice about what we've learned and translated into opinions or actions, we also need to temper those expressions in our interactions with others to avoid the trap of judgments and overstepping our real roles.

Consider:

Do I find ways to honor my own honesty and discoveries in all my relationships?

Are there times when I also may mistake my inner voice for perfect vision and knowledge?

How can I bring more balance into my daily life between my own presence and that of other people and situations?

TWENTY-TWO: Ignorance

At times it may seem that unintentional ignorance is bliss, at least according to the old adage bandied about. However, intentional ignorance by avoiding or denying an issue only prolongs the inherent fallacies and weakness of our position. Choosing to remain ignorant about financial stewardship responsibilities and options by defaulting to excuses such as not being good at math, or money isn't the most important thing in life, or other avoidance expressions simply leads to unbalanced choices in all areas of life. But it is in tackling those areas in our lives that seem to be the most difficult that we really grow and flourish with the greatest rewards.

Consider:

When and why do I avoid financial stewardship review, and what have been some consequences in the past?

What steps can I take to become more knowledgeable and stronger in this important area?

What other parts of my life will also be positively affected as I gain more understanding and knowledge?

TWENTY-THREE: Impact

We've all been given particular gifts and skills to develop and use for our own benefit and that of those around us. Sometimes we know early on what passions we need to follow and other times that awareness comes over time – or at a specific intended time. Whatever your phase in this life, it's important to honor those callings and to figure out what is the best way for yourself to follow through with action. Being an owner of your financial stewardship role is one way to more powerfully impact the action that you take. Whether you choose to allocate monetary resources toward a new goal, make adjustments to other finances, or gain a deeper understanding of how your financial choices affect other areas of your life, being an active steward will strengthen your core foundation and add needed momentum to your pursuit.

Consider:

What limiting thoughts or perceptions around finances do I need to get rid of to make my actions more impactful?

What new energies can I develop to support both my financial and skills stewardship?

How can I better envision the impact I want to have in these focused areas?

TWENTY-FOUR: Indulgence

Abundance is a wonderful gift that we are meant to enjoy fully and share with others around us. But shifting into the perspective that we deserve to indulge ourselves through food, money, clothing, household goods, trips, and a multitude of other items because of hard work or to mask turmoil in our souls becomes a harmful cycle. If we accumulate an excess of items beyond what we truly need and beneficially want, then the accompanying debt, weight, clutter, and unused things are actually anchors that hold us back on our journey. When we notice this situation developing, or perhaps a caring individual brings it to our attention, we then have the opportunity to re-consider why we're taking these particular actions and make adjustments to move toward a healthier, more balanced lifestyle. Since our finances are related to so many of these choices, it's important to include steps to review our financial stewardship in this review.

Consider:

What areas in my life may be influenced right now by acquisition or reward behavior instead of healing and purpose?

How can I begin to take steps to reduce these influences?

What are some supportive resources I can tap to help me move ahead?

TWENTY-FIVE: Integrity

Personal integrity is an important trait that we strive to develop with the greatest honesty for ourselves, and an attribute that we aspire to demonstrate to those around us. This level of honesty also requires that we take a close and dedicated look at how we are managing our financial stewardship responsibilities: are you diligent in expanding your knowledge, thoughtful in the allocation of your monetary resources to match your intentions, and cognizant of how your actions here are impacting those who rely on you? Hiding behind ignorance, fear, random choices, judgment, or overlooking accountability is not part of a truthful, or effective, life. But you always have the chance to change your future by changing your actions and thoughts to reach the integrity we desire.

Consider:

Do I consistently check my actions to see if they are driven by my personal integrity?

Are there certain times when I know deep down that I'm 'cutting corners' in my life?

What situations seem to provide the greatest challenges for me and why?

TWENTY-SIX: Intention

Each of us has chosen to be a personal seeker of enlightenment based on our intention to grow, serve, and flourish in our own particular path. These intentions are extremely powerful beacons that keep us focused and persistent along our journey through all types of experiences and transformations. Healing the past and dreaming the future are reliant upon being thoughtfully and truthfully aware of both our strengths and foibles. And using the resources of angels, spirits, guides, and other energies are incredible gifts to help us continually refine our learning and knowing and move us closer to the understanding we seek.

Consider:

Have I recently reviewed my intentions to measure my progress and integration throughout my life?

How can I reach out more strongly or differently to the many resources who want to help me achieve my thoughtful intentions?

Are my intentions set well to balance growth and effectiveness rather than a distant perfection goal?

TWENTY-SEVEN: Knowledge

Awareness, insight, observation and recognition are all components of knowledge. However, the transformation of basic knowledge into real power comes when we absorb information and concepts into our entire being and intention, making a seamless composition into our inner core. If we mistake retention of facts, explanations, or certain practices as real knowledge, we limit our true experiences and understandings to a surface level...appearing to mimic a level of proficiency or expertise yet really missing the integral message and application in our lives. While we all need to begin our quest with step by step processes and tools, we cannot long remain in someone else's interpretation of knowledge or practice of rituals. We must take the leap into our own discoveries and claim the answers that are inside ourselves.

Consider:

Do I place over-reliance on another's instruction or methodology for certain reasons?

Why is it vital that I look inside myself for motivations and answers?

How can I make chosen rituals and practices more meaningful and thought-filled in my own life?

TWENTY-EIGHT: Legacy

When we were conceived we were gifted with a personal contract for our life here – our inherent knowledge, ties to ancestors, contributions we could make to the world, lessons to be learned, and more. Once we were born, though, outside influences, teachings and energies began to impact our souls and often our personal contracts as well. Later in life, we often assume that our challenges, frustrations, results, and position are simply part of an original defined destiny and we have little to do but struggle on and make do with our present situation. If this is our current mindset we have lost awareness of the beautiful soul connection and potential that were our first gifts of life. When we begin to recognize, acknowledge, and reclaim our universal connection and then learn and heal with the multitude of spirits and guides available to us, we can not only re-enter our initial intentions but actively influence our futures as well. Your legacy can be whatever you decide to create for yourself...financial, charitable, family, or other

Consider:

What resources are available to help me regain awareness and healing so I can claim my intended legacy?

How can I thoughtfully find and explore the path that is appropriate for me at this time?

What do I need to release within myself that could limit or derail the legacy I choose?

TWENTY-NINE: Motivation

Motivation is an infinite cycle involving our intentions, actions, outcomes, and energies. If there is a disruption or break at any of the points during this cycle we begin to lose our focus and momentum, and a period of review and recommitment are necessary to resume the effective path forward. Responsible financial stewardship requires that we bring this level of awareness to our learning and thoughtful decision making in the same way we apply attention to our health, relationships, and lifestyle choices. The temptation to dodge proficiency in our money matters by viewing these as areas for "specialists only" is a siren call that will quickly lead us astray to ignorance, denial, and abdicating decision making.

Consider:

When am I tempted to ignore my financial choices and education?

How can I reconnect my intentions for a thoughtful life with being a good financial steward?

What benefits are there to me and my family in planning ahead and having conversations about our choices and goals?

THIRTY: Myths

Myths exist in legend and lore, tale and fable, parable and tradition. What is repeated often enough may become ingrained in our minds so as to be an indisputable, given truth. While there is a type of comfort in continuing to repeat and rely on phrases generated by others, there is a greater danger that we not only lose our own ability to question and reason through situations but that we ultimately cede our personal outcomes to inaccurate or inappropriate statements. There are many, many financial myths that make the rounds in our lives – from old comments that keep being passed around to new proclamations set forth daily to meet someone else's purposes. Financial stewardship calls us to become involved in gathering information, testing options, tapping solid resources, and evaluating the alternatives that are most beneficial for our particular needs and time.

Consider:

What financial-related statements have I been accepting as given truths without doing my own research and consideration?

Where can I find several sources of respected information and options that I can review and evaluate myself?

How will looking at new perspectives and taking responsibility in my financial stewardship help me achieve my stated intentions and goals?

THIRTY-ONE: Negligence

When we become lax in our care and oversight in various areas of our lives, we not only miss important opportunities but may also actually cause harm to ourselves and others. Being actively involved in life requires a good deal of focused energy and mindfulness. Balancing rest and rejuvenation with active thinking and doing is also a vital calling in a meaningful and effective journey. This balance can be accomplished by periodically reviewing our time, commitments, and intentions to test the direction and synchronization of our path. Being a commendable financial steward also involves this regular review of our financial situation, goals, and decision-making process. As we take the necessary time to consider our resources and their uses, we have the ability to make adjustments and choices that will fuel our long term plans.

Consider:

When was the last time I reviewed my whole financial picture in terms of my intentions and plans?

Are there areas where I'm actually causing, or will cause, harm to myself or family by inattention or inaction to financial matters?

What energies or perceptions do I need to change in myself to more comfortably and actively manage decisions related to money?

THIRTY-TWO: Perception

Perception can run the definition range from awareness and consciousness to judgment and viewpoint. As we move along this scale, our outlook on a person or situation moves from observation and consideration to labeling and defining...a significant change in how flexible and open we are to sensing other options or interpretations. Acknowledging the outcomes and impacts of past experiences is part of our survival and ability to exist in this physical world. But it is only part of our capability and responsibility. How we thoughtfully manage our perceptions with our current actions has a major effect on our future expectations and experiences, so it will serve us well in the long term to compare our perceptions with the intentions we seek to envision and create going forward.

Consider:

In terms of financial stewardship, what assumptions or judgments have I made in the past that may either no longer hold true with different people or changing situations?

Do I need to hold stronger inner guidance or less outer judgment to more fully manage my finances?

How do my money choices and actions differ when I am at different places on the perception scale?

THIRTY-THREE: Preparation

Preparation proceeds action and may take different forms over time. Laying the groundwork, doing your homework, and rehearsing are all phases that are necessary to succeed at your chosen goal – and you may need to switch back and forth between them before taking an actual step forward or making a particular change. Applying the preparation process to your financial stewardship involves the same intention, learning, and consideration themes, and may require some additional discipline to persevere if finances have not previously been a comfortable part of your dialogue before. However, the same concepts of reward and accomplishment apply to the successful transition to financial steward as happens in other areas of your life.

Consider:

When and why do I defer the preparation process in terms of my financial responsibilities and choices?

What intentions and incentives do I have that will help me gain more mastery in this area?

How will my comfort level and quality of my financial decisions increase when I take ownership through more preparation?

THIRTY-FOUR: Priorities

Two key ways to directly evaluate how we manifest our priorities is to look at our calendars and our bank accounts. These indicators show how we are currently spending our valuable time and monetary resources in real terms. If our intention is to fully apply and focus our resources toward those areas we proclaim to be important to us, then we seek to spend the vast majority of our time and funds in these ways. However, without making conscious choice our ongoing companion, it is easy to find ourselves derailed into other thoughts and activities that take up our time and money without returning the benefits and outcomes that are truly desired and meaningful in our lives. This can be the case in the quality or type of relationships we have, how we allocate our monetary earnings to various categories, and where our time and precious energies are spent.

Consider:

Am I actually putting my resources into the priorities that enrich my life or have I fallen into a less considered daily routine?

What is not in sync between my calendar, bank account, and the priorities I maintain?

How can I more thoughtfully adjust and balance these areas to help me attain the personal and communal goals I seek?

THIRTY-FIVE: Provision

Whether you are putting together provisions for a journey, allocating provisions in daily life, or making a provision within your financial legacy, all of these actions require taking stock of your current resources, locating or creating necessary new ones, and determining how they will best be used to meet your goal. Your inventory combined with new tools and a thoughtful plan comprise the approach needed to ensure you have sufficient resources to achieve the outcome you seek. And as you do your part with planning and being a steward of your provisions, you will find that the Spirit or Universe contributes additional resources and guidance to match your efforts and application. The type and amount of each resources we individually need and receive varies depending on our intentions, insights, and vision.

Consider:

Am I good steward of the resources I currently have and so may genuinely request additional universal provisions in support of my endeavors?

How does trust, gratitude, and initiative tie into the gifts and resources that are available to me?

What can I do to better balance planning with awareness of opportunities?

THIRTY-SIX: Purpose

Setting forth your desire, intent, wish, and aspiration are all expressions of the purpose you truly want to have within your life. While only a certain portion choose to pursue the area of finances and stewardship on a career basis, we can all benefit from dedicating some time to understanding and including thoughtful decisions about these areas in our own lives... just as making time for physical exercise, spiritual study, and other activities influence and enrich our lives. And for life on planet Earth, being financially literate is a necessary component to integrating the use of our value and resources toward the other desired purposes in life such as relationships, legacies, personal passions, and more. When you accept the role of financial steward as part of your complete being, you have the power and ability to effectively use money as the tool that it is – not merely as an object to be labeled as good or bad and treated accordingly in simplistic terms.

Consider:

Am I taking the time I need to develop myself as a steward for the resources I have been given?

How can I better incorporate my financial decisions with the purposes I want for my life?

What steps can I take to strengthen my skills as a financial steward and further influence the effectiveness of my path?

THIRTY-SEVEN: Reflection

Taking the time to look back and identify the various events that contributed to where we are now is a very important part to figuring out our future priorities and actions. Doing this can be a bit challenging to keep honesty and intention in focus, however this time is our chance to make adjustments, change course, or move closer to our potentials in a whole variety of ways. Stepping away from a hectic daily schedule periodically puts us back in touch with the true peace of mind and comfort we feel when we know we're following the path that is best for us at the time. As the steward of your financial resources, you are the only one who can determine whether you are developing the knowledge you need for good decisions and if you are taking responsibility for the direction and type of your choices.

Consider:

When I take time to meditate and reflect, do I give adequate time to my financial education and choices, and how they affect the rest of my life?

When and why do I minimize this area of my life in comparison to meditations on physical health, friendships, work, children, and other topics?

How can I bring more clarity and focus to coordinating financial stewardship with its influence on these other parts of my life?

THIRTY-EIGHT: Responsibility

Being truly responsible in any area of our life – whether with children, home, work, or health - means that we're taking full ownership for our role in a situation. When we've made a particular commitment and vowed to move ahead with strong intention, in spite of internal challenges or perceived obstacles, we have an amazing ability to channel our strength, ingenuity, vision, and persistence to meet that goal. How often have we looked back at a situation and thought 'I had no idea how to get this done, but I was determined'? In retrospect, we can see how our own initiative and help from others (including universal energies) came together to create a wonderful outcome. Although financial knowledge and competency may not be at the top of your personal interest level, nonetheless it's an integral part of our relationships, raising children, envisioning our future lives on earth, and much more. Developing financial stewardship abilities is not just something 'nice for other people to do'…it's vital to the complete picture of your life and goals.

Consider:

How will being more responsible, and responsive, in finances affect the rest of my life?

What steps can I take today, this week, this year, to achieve the changes I want to experience?

How do I balance my actions proportionally with the responsibility others need to bring to the table?

THIRTY-NINE: Sustenance

When we receive real sustenance – be it food, water, sleep, support, or other form – we feel a sense of fullness and peace that is a true blessing. In contrast, acquiring or accumulating items or attention to prop up our egos and unaddressed fears and insecurities leaves us with a hollow, short term feeling that must be addressed time and time again in order for us to keep functioning. When we find ourselves in a constant state of unease, frustration, indecision, or tension, that is a strong sign to step out of our current mode and find a better way to focus and prioritize our lives. As we quiet our bodies and minds and become again more open to the real messages we are receiving, the positive energies and support that we really need are available to help us make sense of our situation and provide guidance in moving toward greater balance and insight.

Consider:

Am I using my financial resources to meet defined goals or am I spending on extra things that simply end up giving me a temporary lift?

Do I have a multitude of toys or tools that are used only infrequently and really end up taking more time and stress to maintain and organize?

How has my spending over the past six months or year or longer supported the main goals and visions I have for my life?

FORTY: Time

Our time is one of the most precious commodities we have and can offer to other people and causes. Likewise, the time that others spend with us – or possibly take from us – is a significant part of this equation. Sometimes it seems hard to place a concrete value on our time for ourselves, and so it's also sometimes given little thought by those who seek our attention – regardless of their intentions. It's important to actively engage in some thoughtful consideration of the value of our time on a regular basis to best align our energies and activities with our best purposes. When we honestly determine our own value and priorities then we can communicate those much more clearly to those around us…and also make more consistent and meaningful contributions with both our time and money. Financial stewardship intertwines with so many other areas of our life and periodically reviewing all these interactions will generate rewards beyond the obvious.

Consider:

When I look at my calendar, is my time being spent with the people, activities, and quality of interaction that I really do want?

What can I adjust with my perception of the value of my time that will make my life's contributions more meaningful and effective?

How can I develop new paradigms surrounding my value of time for both myself and those around me?

FORTY-ONE: Transition

Transition times in our lives provides opportunities for growth, evolution and transformation. Sometimes, though, we resist these periods and instead respond with anger, fear, denial, resistance, or procrastination and our lives then become even more unsettled, uncertain, and unsatisfactory. As we consciously pause and re-view transition as the antidote to idleness, sameness, and stagnation, we open ourselves to positive soul searching and thoughtful decision making. In those times where we face financial challenges, it can be easy to magnify our fears and concerns about how to make provision for our physical needs and obligations while we align our purpose and future vision. There are countless resources available to us for guidance from both earthly and universal planes to help us keep our current situation in better perspective. However, it's equally important that we take personal responsibility for learning, evaluating and preparing our personal finances so we have some options and flexibility available to support us.

Consider:

Why is it vital for me to take stock of my resources and make informed plans before transition times happen?

How will being prepared in this way make uncertain times easier for me and those around me?

How does my own preparation affect the assistance I can ask for and receive from the universe?